Manifestation

By
Amunet Wolfbane

ISBN 978-0-6151-8528-6

First Edition

Front cover art by Amunet Wolfbane

Back cover art is a portrait of Amunet Wolfbane that was originally created
and gifted to her back in 2003 by the artist Christopher W. Price.
Studio|chris · http://www.studiochris.us
Blog · http://www.studiochris.us/blog
Shop · http://www.studiochris.us/shop

This book is dedicated to my family.

To those that have gone to Summerland:

My Grandmother, Ruth
Her voice spans the ethers to find me, giving me strength.

My Grandfather, Calvin
He was the calm in the storm and the light in the dark.

My Dad, Michael Wayne
He was truly my world and I still miss him everyday.

And to those of you that still walk with me through life:
Thank you all for loving me. I love you too.

My Grandmother, Mary Ellen
for always comforting me and being willing to listen.

My Grandfather, Henry Ford
for your quiet strength and ability to see me as I truly am.

My Mother, Kathryn and Stepfather, Earl
for loving me even when I am impossible to understand
and giving me the foundation to be secure in who I am.

My Siblings, Jason, Matt and Aymee
It would take a book to commend the wonders of you all.
You are the glue that holds me together. Thank you.
I wouldn't trade one second of my life with any of you.

My Nephew and Niece, Jacob and Jessica
You are the future of our family, the joy and sunshine.
Both of you fill my world with all things pure and good.
I look forward to watching you grow and succeed in life.

My Best Friends, Ron and Lisa
You know my flaws, my depths and most of my secrets and yet you've
both stayed with me through my madness, believing in me, even when I
didn't believe in myself. I'm not really sure why you do. But I can't
imagine finishing life without the two of you. Thanks for being you.

Author's Foreword

This book is a collection of my thoughts on many things of interest in my life. While some may say it is not up to par in poetic form, they are pieces of my heart, my spirit and soul. You might say at one point this poetry saved my life, allowing my thoughts to unravel and soar from my pen to paper.

There are no categories in this book, as I believe there really are no categories to life. Life is life and what we make our lives to be. In this fashion, this book is compiled a bit randomly, as my thoughts tend to be. You will find love, sadness, fantasy, heartbreak, personal issues, society issues and lots of spirituality. I hope you enjoy them as much as I've enjoyed writing them and sharing them over the years.

Welcome
to
Manifestation

By

Amunet Wolfbane

Mystery Writings
Written July 25th, 2005

In the emptiness of my mind, I sought what I should do
to mend my heart, to live my life and heal all of my wounds
And as my mind fluttered, pictures started to form
revealing hidden words to me and thus my poetry formed

I don't know where it comes from, a little pain, some joy and sadness.
Sometimes a dream, a vent or rage or even a glimpse at my madness
At times I let you delve inside, deep into the depths of my soul
But most the time it's just fantasies that never have been told.

I simply put my pen to paper as my hand moves on it's own
and hope that it all makes sense when it's ready to be shown
But should my paper wield ancient symbols or forbidden things
sacred its kept or meets the fire setting it off upon angel's wings

For prophecy, does often speak displaying tongues of olden ways
not meant to meet the mundane world in such passionate displays
So now you know my secret muse, the voice that spurs the mystery
of words spun into poetic form from my hand, for the world to see

Hallowed Hollow

Written August 24th, 2007

Entrance me, solid conviction, within hallowed seeds of light
derived within mind fantasies, coursing manifestation to life

And there I shall beckon kindly frothy memories, spun in silk
parchment savored antiquities reigning posh against my quill

Beneath veils of ecliptic lovers within moments of their touch
quite entranced, I stare in awe awaiting their ardor to combust

11

Dragon Fly
Written July 9th, 2006

In slumber, I weep rivers of humanity
Recycling love, defeated honor, trust
Lost innocence preserving exiled souls
in tranquil weavings of nature's womb

Lucid images of resurrection seethe
beneath the sun's guide, life's tease
Promising acceptance of happiness
in shadow forged bridges of reality

Here I fly uninhibited, quite untouched
between edges of dying races and earth
Weaving wonders which shall go unseen
by eyes blind to the process of spirituality

Drowning in their ignorance, their denial
my body lifeless, its luster dims to cease
Forgotten in the turmoil of selfish chaos
I transcend beyond this world, I am free

Luminous Echoes
Written April 25th, 2006

Whisper to me, something broken, breathless nothings on the wind
secrets held within your fortress soul guarded in shattered whims

Reach beyond material realms, claim the twilight of denial
twisting fate to manifestation upon the curves of indigo spirals

And there I shall embrace you stealing away all shards of pain
until you weep golden tear drops forgetting sorrows of yesterday

Embracing Indigo
Written May 11th, 2005

My weary mind reels, seeking release
upon the indigo spirals of astral streams
Silently awaiting the moment in time
when my body rests and my soul shall fly

Sitting in the shadows of a lone candlelight
my eyes lightly close, letting Kundalini rise
Mentally chasing the rainbow, from earth to sky
I breathe deeply, relaxing both body and mind

In moments I glimpse, beyond white light
taunting me softly, through my third eye
Lavender glows, deepening in brilliant shades
taking me into the serenity of indigo's haze

Waves of spirituality, steadily lighten my frame
releasing stressful holds of the mundane
soothing me to the very essence of my soul
as I sink into the visions of my beloved indigo

Enlightened I travel, uninhibited or afraid
through the mysteries of the Akashic plane
at one with the universe, on a path of light
quickened with energies of the sacred divine

Etheric mist, carries me gingerly back down
to settle within my physical body's bounds
empowered I rise, ready to face a new day
illuminated with the glow of Indigo's embrace

Elysian Absolute
Written May 8th, 2005

Escaping, I rise from the ashes of life's hollow grip
Soaring through visions upon the azure mist of light
Partaking of the essence of all that's revealed there
reclaiming the sacred power that has long been mine

Empowered, I land silently, upon the rich soil of earth
raising my arms, feeling the power of the great divine
knowing that I am the essence of the sun and moon
awaiting the quickening of all that I am, combined

Slowly I begin to spin, bathed within a golden light
remembering, what was once forgotten over time
My spirit free, energies stirring me within euphoria
I reel within the powers of the elements intertwined

I am the whisper of hope, the void, the alchemic change
fire, lightning, passion and love, the raging winds and rains
I am the trees and leaves, the thunderstorms and streams
rainbows, lightning, rocks and seas, I am all and no-thing

The stars and sunrise meeting the night serenely, I am
laughter, sorrow, life and death, the power to understand
the flowers in bloom, winter's kiss, autumn's change, I am
waterfalls and butterflies, the warmth beneath the sand

I am supreme enchantment, beauty, chaos and serenity
the healer, seeker and sorcerer, the wizard and the witch
I am the manifestation of my desires, paths and dreams
the teacher of mystery, the student of life, the furlong wish

At one with the universe, I am as I should be, once more
cleansed of negative debris that had stained me in this life
awaiting the next lesson, along the path I have chosen
I am a pentacle of power, an obelisk of divinity's light

The Lone Christmas Bulb (For Jacob)

Written July 2003 – A rough original version that I still cannot bear to change.

Today the house was quiet the day, just dragging by
depression had filled me up until I often wanted to die
Just as I thought to go to bed and hide the day away
My brother called to ask me to watch the kids today

The kids arrived in a frenzy, I thought "what have I done"
But my nephew paused to look at me, leaned over and kissed me once
My niece took his hand and led him to the living room
to watch Christmas stories while they played and sang tunes

Suddenly she ran up to me, leaning close to my ear
"You've no Christmas tree, Santa won't come this year"
I'd given the large tree away and hundreds of ornaments too
But I had a small one in the garage that I thought I could still use

I dragged the little tree in, where to put it, I didn't know
my niece dragged in a TV tray "Look aunt T, here we go"
I had one box of ornaments left, mostly old sentimental ones
My nephew dug through the box. It's the Christmas bulb he wants

I strung the lights and watched in amazement as he worked
he took each ornament in his hand studied it and carefully hung it up
I'd hand him the lone Christmas bulb but he'd put it right back down
my niece and I just watched him while he moved all around

We thought the ornaments were hung but there was just one more
My nephew had the Christmas bulb, It was full of snow and a rose
He carried that bulb so tenderly and placed it into my hand
Tears sprung into my eyes as I watched this tiny little man

He looked me in the eye and kissed me softly on the cheek
then said to me so softly "you put it on the tree"
I burst into to tears as I hung it, my nephew wrapped around my leg
He hardly speaks, he's barely here, but today was my lucky day

I bought that Christmas bulb the year that he was born
He rode in the cart and held it as we shopped and brought it home
I think he somehow knew it and just wanted me to see
that even if he's locked away he still remembers me

I know I'll never forget again to put up the Christmas tree
as long as that bulb remains, hope shall live inside of me

15

Little Fox (For Jessica)
Written August 19th, 2007

Dark amber mirrors violet stars
too familiar, too in-depth to probe
Tortures to a womb, never used
captive in fascination's steady hold

Fingers curl within my open palm
age removed, smaller than my own
Yet there, the crooked digit smiles
awaiting my lead to tour my home

A child's laughter fills the magic attic
a room dreams always seek to fill
She talks to spirits, quite enchanted
questioning me on gems and spells

Ancestors echo around joined hands
their rays of light, saying "told you so"
as I relish in the delight of teaching
a child that could easily be my own

Leaning towards me we nose kiss
her daddy's calling, they need to go
I hear him whisper "she's just like you"
and from my brother's eyes tears flow

I used to pray for her to come to me
while wasting years in lover's lies
but now I know, the best of me lives
sharing knowledge through blood lines

Impregnated
Written July 6th, 2007

Fevered waters proclaim faith
as innocence awaits sparks of humanity

Eyes of Jupiter
Written June 20th, 2005

Eyes of Jupiter
leak tears

Sweet sensations
cascading waves
in a rain of golden caresses

Heightening the senses
quickening intuition
moving you, in its rhythm

Lost
in a timeless dance
where the euphoria of love
is the ballerina

Twirling in hues,
wonders stimulating
endorphins
until passion peaks

Drowning you
in the bliss of abundance
awaiting the capture
of your heart, entranced

Within the happiness
of solar stars

Catching My Breath
Written May 25th, 2005

There's air here. I'm breathing.

Breathing in the scent of the trees,
as the birds chirp their songs at 5 A.M.,
not caring that the rest of the world sleeps,
or that I am standing in their midst,
silently, trying to float away.

Yes, I'm awake, breathing,
as the geese fly overhead,
bellowing loud tones, in the light blue sky,
gliding upon a faint, cool breeze
that soothes the senses.

Morning dew, softly touches me
as my bare feet linger in freshly cut grass,
easing down to feel the earth's essence,
as it claims the heaviness that I've wore,
like a suit of armor.

Eyes closed, I lean my head back,
feeling the wind touch me, as I breathe,
wondering why nature has eluded me,
or if perhaps I just closed it off,
not wanting to feel anything for awhile.

But now...
now I'm breathing,
breathing crisp air, hearing voices of nature,
feeling the energies rise through my feet,
as I watch a deer stare and a bunny hop,
through a neighborhood of holly and pine.

And I ask myself,
surrounded by the serenity of this place,
when it was that I had forgotten to breathe,
or hear the birds sing, or even feel the grass,
when did I forget, that I am a part of it all?
I don't remember, I only know that I barely lived.

And now...now I breathe.

Nature's Breath
Written August, 2007

Autumn feathers voice specks of time
Silk innuendos to mundane eyes

Enlightened, beauties cultivate elemental cascades
Their mischief...cleansing rain

Cotton Blued
Written August 19th, 2007

I cotton to you
under Life's x-ray
displaying vulnerable edges
in numerous seeds

Pulling so gingerly,
an attached energy
willed into voids of
impoverished emotions

My integrated intentions
segregate in your spindle
rotating so carelessly
in irrelevant blood lines

Tainted fingertips
marring wombs of perfection
in palm shadowed victories
of self proclaimed saints

Wear my threads
loosely upon spider veins
they share your hollow
but my core, reseeds

Soul Dust
Written July 7th, 2007

Magnified snippets
of secluded thoughts
mesh with elegance

Manifesting dreams

Complete Without Sound
Written July 29th, 20007

Cross legged serenity claims me
a harness feathered in indigo lights

A silhouette, quite crystalline
wielding sapphires invade my mind

Slender fingers start palm dancing
nirvana rising in kindred souls

The high, natural, a cool essence
elemental fires moving to forge

Unity bound without restraints
kismet connections completely sound

Divinity pales to transcending minds
seeking perfection in other realms

Eclipse
Written July 5th, 2007

Heavenly teases unite with persistence,
golden splendor kissing silvery beams.
A moment of pure bliss too brilliant to be seen,

Kissing Divinity
Written January 28th, 2007

Cinders, once emanating gold
 suffocate emotions in defiance
an adept taint of healing woes
that try in vain to cause demise

Underestimated, silence conquers
seemingly passive traits smolder
Indigo softly breeching the flesh
devouring dis-ease, untouchable

Tentacles caressing Ra, feeding
How his kiss loves to nourish
stroking waves, rebirth's desire
embracing indigo, entwines gold

Fused in balance a warrior stands
victorious, a healer resurrected
a being of light, un-tethered
claiming a power older than time

Gnarled fingertips hold no threat
mass hysteria, but a fading whisper
amongst deafening roars of release
as I walk within serenity, divine

Collective Experience
Written July 8th, 2007

Hap-hazards cultivate life's cobblestones
Crevices of mystery leave vast impressions

Velocity
Written August, 2007

Unknown templates
 mark destiny

Stark illuminations
 peaking against crushed velvet
with torn seams

Allure is fancied
a melody too rich to despise in gender

Yet, you sink into blind travels

Stagnant
Written July 8th, 2007

Knowledge quivers within shallow minds
Un-sated desires denying life's key

Ancient Oak
Written July 7th, 2007

Breathe, she will breathe.
Entwine in her harmony.

Secrets whispered on winds,
embedded in your soul.

Panoramic vision is required

Smoldering Sandalwood
Written May 14th, 2005

Charcoal smolders within the temple
illuminated with the warmth of candlelight
as I sprinkle the fine tan powder down
letting its aroma fill the room and sanctify

Silver antique chimes, softly play their tune
while dancing in serenity, to the wind's caress
Clarity coming to mind, as I breath the scent
wafting from the tan burner's smoking vents

Cross legged, upon on a wooden floor of tan
as spiritual vibrations rise steadily higher
through mist of incense, I softly begin to chant
focused upon the intent of that which I desire

Lost within the euphoria of divine energies
built within the cone of power, awaiting release
I light tan parchment, setting my spell free
raising my arms, with the words "so mote it be"

Whitesmoke's Violation
Written June 12th, 2005

Peace eludes me
No longer, can I close my eyes
Night's solitude lost
to fantasia of the mind

Masculine swirls conjure
Sheens of white
mingling with grey
Unwelcome advances
caress in sexual ways

Heavy emotions of lust
shower, like static cling
Bodies of mist taunting
probing my thighs
Distorted faces, whispering

Against my back, it melds
burrowing in silken hair
My body surrenders
as it claims me, my
mind screaming in despair

Attached, it lingers
throughout the night
Shape-shifting into men I've longed for
as though winning my adoration
were his quest of mind

Never realizing
my love, he never shall gain
In denying my freedom
dreams of romantic notions
merely turned to hate

Lost in whitesmoke's lustful games

Infidelity
Written August, 2007

Adrenaline permeates receptors
vanquishing serenity's tether

A Gemini response to unsavory
innuendos, breaking holy union

Sightings
Written August, 2007

Fog induced hysteria peaks obscure amber.
A revelation of death wavering in echoes of reality.

Self Expression is Golden
Written July 7th, 2007

Creativity is necessary
Self expression, undeniable
Incomparably golden, always on display

Artistic endeavors maintain souls

Dancing Con Amore
Written June 3rd, 2005

They called her Sapphire, as she danced
beneath the glowing stars and moon
Twirling, lost within a world of fantasy
swaying to the beat of her own tune

We stared in awe, through the gardens
to where she ruled the fountain's floor
Holding arms around a mystery lover
slightly tilting her head, con amore

Deep velvet blue clung like cellophane
against the curves of her aging youth
So alluring against Mediterranean skin
kissed by sunlight's bronzing hues

Golden elegance, glimmered daintily
from the silken hollow of her throat
Displaying a gem, much like her eyes
smoldering sapphires, carrying hope

Mingling through the night, we watched
while the party thrived, she danced on
No one seemed to know her true name
or care that she really danced alone

As her laughter filled the air, at dawn
we wondered, who'd take her home
Turning just in time, to catch a glimpse
of Sapphire fading into marble stones

Labradorite Smiles
Written October 13th, 2005

Saline leaks, undisturbed
Alone effort to erase a frown
beneath vacant, lying eyes
defying sensuality, unbound

Closed, she waits in silence
refusing a scream to be held
Against the winds of change
within her soul, it echoes well

The world smiling to her face
Casting cruelty, against her back
She reaches out, they back away
fearing her poisonous attack

And they wonder, how they wonder
why she hides away, all by herself
Yet no one took the time to ask
or look into her eyes or try to help

Power surges in her essence
striving to heal a broken heart
Ebbed with painful vengeance
of loneliness that won't depart

Magic revived, becomes reality
the dream of love, just a bane
In the empty hollowed shell
of human touch, denied in vain

Quickening comes within the light
The light of lights, divinity's call
and she'll answer with sultry eyes
mysterious indigo, watching it all

Walking amongst, those that shun
misunderstood in their ignorance
Labradorite smiles, await the day
they come to call with their request

Seeking a healer, as the universe shifts
when their minds bleed with self contempt

27

Sightings
Written August, 2007

Fog induced hysteria
peaks obscure amber

A revelation of death
wavering in echoes of reality

Sacred Lovers
Written September 5th, 2005

Sacred lovers within cool waters,
embrace serenity.

Echoes of wonder stir wind songs,
cleansing their naked bodies.

Rejuvenation comes in embers,
seeking lunar waves.

Energies meld timeless, uninhibited,
crystalline sheen, golden silver haze.

Sultry enchantments, breathless spells,
churning sands, silently seething.

Elements entwine with indigo spirals,
embracing divinity.

Caresses pulsate electricity,
manifesting will mundane eyes don't see.

Ecstasy's sighs meet quivering flesh
upon ritual release.

Veiled Flesh
Written January 31st, 2007

Severed hearts.

Spirit's simplicity uninhibited by moral eyes;
steal kisses, yielding in passions wings.

Encircled, complete, esteemed only to their own.
Awaiting balance, they cry bewildered.

Phantasm explodes

Sapphire's Elixir
Written July 10th, 2007

Demure sapphires feign elusive gazes,
claiming a sultry heart with disarming smiles.

Vixen heat ignites.
Captivation maintained in combustion un-denied.

Empowered Stance
Written August, 2007

Feminine wiles.

Etheric orbs of desire, undisputedly sublime.

Power personified.

Ubiquitous Love
Written August 5th, 2007

Unknown caverns excite me;
their elementals beckoning the essence of my soul

There I caress Aether so boldly;
erasing negative illusions with solid temptations,

A creation of self, in control

Silver Silhouettes
Written February 23rd, 2006

How profound it is that your words stretched out upon my tongue,
releasing to the winds a song of enchantment.

Carrying the essence of whims denied only by society's captivation
Manifesting charcoal dreams into the reality of time

And yet our eyes never met as our souls meshed in silence
riding indigo stardust in places flesh never exists.

Static Longing
Written September 22nd, 2007

Electric blue told the story,
saturated in cosmic hues.

Dilated pupils remember,
whiskers, love transfused.

Phantom Sighs
Written February 1st, 2007

Fascination breeds regret against swollen breasts
feeding a soul, once lost with timeless happiness

Reality, ever so cruel in its quest for demise
echoes pain in our limbs as ethers quake, sublime

A tear holds this image, golden lovers entwined
as silver cords sever guardians mourn lives

Regret breeds fascination during sleepless nights
as we search our dreams listening to phantom sighs

Pheromones
Written July 15, 2007

Mundane heartbeats mesmerized by nature's perfume.
Enlightenment's joke on reality

Dancing Between the Veils
Written April 21st, 2005

Musky scents of heated flesh lingers
steadily, as though around me it belongs
Taunting my senses, swirling fantasies
of our bodies melding in solitude, as one

Soul searching, I yearn to trust you
longing to share with you secrets of my realm
Though I reached out, you denied reality
and the consummation of our true selves

Loneliness begins to seek places inside
where their bitter shadows never peeked
Drawing gloom through open windows
like a magnet, stealing euphoria from me

Captivation seems irrelevant now
mundane prisons stifling the beauty of us
Egos clashing with hidden emotions
games of the mind forming unquenched lust

Sideways glances with husky breaths
like invitations, to once again join the dance
Taunt passions to rise within my hollow heart
but your arrogance killed any emotions I had left

Comforting enchantments shall finally claim me
Your essence banished in mysterious ways
Unimpressed by your power, immune to charms
I'll walk empowered and you shall regret every game

Blue Morning
Written December 5, 2007

It pains me in dawn's silence,
cool sheets, calling your name,
As I practice ghost whispers
against a dirty window pane.

Eyes closed, I fancy the vixen
seen in eyes of men of old,
wandering into wrinkled hands,
paving valleys to yet behold.

And here within the solace
of tainted tears, choking my eyes,
I relinquish the savior, loneliness,
to face the day without a smile.

Spiritual Allegiance
Written January 1st, 2007

Tainted sheets shield the aftermath, drowning the sorrow of these days
As though the blood of innocence did not stain humanity's crusade

Life forces stagnate in their denial. Hearts seethe bitter, so enraged.
Primal urges evolve to encompass greedy reality, showing no shame

Such grandeur in defense of lives soiled by society's pearly whites
How pristine the world's become feigning ignorance to blind eyes

Once I watched, slowly choking trying to breathe blackened air
Testing each aspect of my faith, wondering where I disappeared

Traveling spirals I found my soul encircled in light, it awaited me
Unchained, restored, I now emerge defying judgments cast by society

Darkness shall not stake a claim nor misconceptions of human beings
The truth lies with knowledge gained when open minds take the time to see

Ghostly Caresses of a Past Life
Written October 23rd, 2004

In the silence of solemn moments
his caress comes to chill my flesh
as his spirit seeks for me to hear

Tormenting the essence of my soul
pain clenching my heart, bringing tears
releasing the loneliness of this life

As the curtains billow like sails in the wind
I gaze upon a ghostly silhouette near the door
knowing his coming is a universal sign

I remember our love, pure and untainted
it spans universal tides like a pirate now
turning it's blade into my devastated heart

As I yearn for the great love we once shared
I beg upon sorrow's whispers for him to leave
praying to extinguish the memories of us

Perhaps he beckons me beyond this world
to ease the breaking of my heart and join him
in a realm only seen through enlightened eyes

For he knows, as I have known many years
my path here shall take me many places
but another love to claim me, I shall never find

Dismissing Love's Ardor
Written May 27th, 2006

Our union shall never be

Discontented, it stirs
the humanity of me
a widow's silent song
trapped like sewage
with nowhere to go

Passion its only savior
sheer will, focused desire
a desire to break free
past the flesh that stains
the acid spirit I contain

Elusive, to the solution
an embrace of true love
I defy its beckoning
its lie of human touch
to ignite internal fires

For I have faced it
head on with open arms
only to wallow in denial
the denial that I wasted
in the weakness of fools

I am too powerful for you

Omnipresent
Written July 26th, 2007

Worldly regrets, severed

Love's breath wavers in sublime affirmation
As silver cord adventures transcend mundane ties

Pivoting on Perfection's high

After-bite
Written July 8th, 2007

Festered ambitions
immortalize toxicity

Gangrene holidays
in spores of reality

Incandescent Orbs
Written July 19th, 2007

Relics of lives past undermine reality,
pestering rebirth from mind stems.
A cultivation of spirit survival, enhanced
within a seers path to enlightenment;
through mirrored doorways of soul.

Prelude to Nothing
Written October 6th, 2005

Whirlwinds captivate the senses
soaring minds beyond reality
immortalizing stolen moments
in waves of Akashic streams

Embracing images beckon
stirring passions and fantasies
leaving hearts lone and cold
in the aftermath of day dreams

Where flesh is all that's truly seen

Vibrations of Nations
Written August 5th, 2007

Cobblestones etch time in tiny crevices of light
marking a chaos too expansive to view.
Poised as society's foundation,
pelted in debris of a million shoes.

Recorded clicks, demented woes,
laughter, sorrow, lust and rage
all written indentations of life;
battered with secrets, unrevealed
accepted by Earth's pitiful face,

Forgotten Avenues
Written December 7, 2007

There must have been a symphony
masturbating mind wars to heart songs
as smoke ringlets filled the room.
For I lost myself within the echo of keys
waiting just one more moment for you.

Tears never surfaced in my spider eyes
leaking their onyx down my cheeks.
Nor did my chest clench with violent pain
as reality announced chartreuse hues
spreading its veiled poison around me.

No, my perfect lips just feigned a smile
to white noise in blue jeans passing by
As the crescendo heightened center stage
I stomped your memory into mahogany
finding new beginnings in sapphire eyes

Hindsight Never Lies
Written July 7th, 2007

Las Vegas reigns in youth.
Sexual prowess a safe seduction
empowering false hopes
when time seems eternal

Post graduation insecurities
chase lost puppy love with
extremities of whiskey sour
being the courage of choice

Until social etiquette demands
menial transgressions unite
un-welcomed reality checks
thrusting forefront, survival

Unnecessary drama dissipates
self awareness seeks serenity
and the soul longs a companion
to breach solitary contempt

Staring through pheromone veils
we choose from the cesspool
gorgeous bodies of shallow form
leaving gilded spirits unknown

Evolution surpasses life's disdain
elderly memoirs haunt to fade
wondering, were we truly loved
heart pains reveal a gilded face

Gypsy Death Ritual
July 17th, 2005

Rhythmic beneath the moonlight
Gypsy dances commence
benzoin fireworks rising'
stirring the ritual of the dead

Thunder stirs forth vengeance
quickening consecrated soil
ancestors answer summons
ascending within their corpse

Lacquered marble's sparkle
enchants the beasts of the night
guardians solid in victory
heal the tribes wounded pride

Stench of decaying limbs linger
upon the wind's poison breath
revealing mysteries of misery
hazing a psyche of dread

Rewards served upon a rapist
denying the right of sanctity
upon the innocence of a maiden
fallen asleep beneath a tree

Formaldehyde dreams forsaken
in screams of hellish delight
shadowing suffocation of life
within the immortality of time

Gypsy ancestors descend
closing the ritual of the dead
as wicked festivities reign
beneath a full moon spent

Media Travesty
Written July 13th, 2007

Denounced perfection stains artistic value
demoralizing threads of lifelong dreams

Animated Gesture
Written July 8th, 2007

Velvet curtains follow tendril driven silhouettes
weeping porcelain tears upon mahogany's grain

Adaptations of denial
trapped midstream in ballerina shoes

Witch Berry Glide
Written May 17th, 2006

Belladonna speak to me in the twilight of the morn
of love gone and life forgot as I strain to face the dawn

My eyes caress your petals knowing answers lie within
I partake of your essence taking flight upon the wind

Warriors whisper so softly taunting echoes, once lost
Shall it be your will's whim, quicken or cease my heart

Belladonna speak to me in the twilight of the morn
and there I make my vow with Hecate once more

Serpent of Lust
Written May 19th, 2005

Acid dripping from my eyes
eating away once silken flesh
Hides the tears you'll never see
beneath a mask you won't forget

Though razors cut my tongue
in torture of the truth it holds
Never shall it yield the words
that you await to be foretold

A prelude to absolutely nothing
is all seductive efforts can yield
for nothing you can do or say
has the power to bend my will

Resurrection's Tears
Written May 7th, 2006

Trials gain nothing when insanity reigns
enlightened tears streak humanity's face
Forces of power waste precious time
healing wounds of drones lost in denial

Maid, Mother and Crone timeless and strong
singe the corridors as darkness again calls
Dragon's breath ablaze in defense of the earth
prohibit its destruction in the wake of rebirth

Men deemed Gods in ignorance of their race
Though empowered, swirl within vanity's game
The bliss of euphoria, simply sealing their fate
Their fall shall be swift and the Ancients await

Backlash
Written July 7th, 2007

Materialism,
Society's claim to fame

Pristine smiles
for plastic personas

Poverty stricken
meets heaven first

Snow Angel Flashbacks
Written August 5th, 2007

White fantasy dictates resolutions
forcing the inner child out to play
It wonders how long to stretch
in rebirth's corridor of innocence

Limbs assess nature's boundaries
Smooth anticipations for lost souls
Reaching for puberty of life, not form
in secrets of earth's hibernation alone

Lying in memories of spines, quilt lined
A smile's chain reaction never dies

Kundalini
Written July 4th, 2007

Subliminal fantasies
  wreak internal chaos

As spasmodic vapor
  penetrates reality

Cherub Affections
Written December 13, 2007

Tiny wings flutter…

An exercise in heat extraction,
fornicating shadows of love
against a wounded aura

How jaded I'd become
without his constant feathering
for affectionate attentions.

Twirling in regret
through flesh ridden pleasure
I sought an ego's romance

Finding love exists
only in a realm too brilliant
for dull eyes to venture

Beneath tiny wings, fluttering

Virtual Nips Reality

Written August 8th, 2007

Though stale, it mattered
those whispers of hope
lingering in dawn's rays
wiping my sleepy eyes

Somehow there, I was alive
eyes closed, mind lurking
feeling secure moments
in warm lingering dreams

How shattered I became
losing tethers of fantasy
false aftermaths caving
in spite I can't understand

Sometimes, I watch you
oblivious to my true depth
still wishing to be accepted
in a world I don't belong to

I'd like to claim innocence
just once, wishing it true
but I know deep in my soul
on some level, I love you

And somewhere in loneliness
part of you reached for me too
two flukes entrapped in dreams
nipping edges of virtual reality

Unconditional Savior
Written April 9th, 2006

Timeless love, our destiny
bittersweet circles of past lives
clinging to a memory of hearts
relived beyond the speed of light

Awaken to enlightenment
upon the path you seek
I would die most gladly
for your spiritual release

Silver cords, align to venture
Indigo spirals, serenity's waves
chaos is but a memory
of souls lost in passion wake

To you, I solemnly plea
eternal pledges, ancient vows
that mundane ties be severed
so you soar, without my bonds

The Purest Embrace
Written August 8th, 2005

Acid tears against silken cheeks faced the darkened moon
asking why love had never come to embrace such tender flesh

And as that flesh fell to the earth in cascades of glowing hues
only silence answered its cries for its soul ascended to the moon

Talisman of my Mind
Written August 6th, 2005

Gazing out of body
beyond the great divine
I seek the answers of life
within the talisman of my mind

Elemental colors etched
in seas of wondrous beings
traveling roads unexplored
beyond logic's reasoning

Balance implemented
in waves of silken swirls
as enlightenment caresses
veils of the mundane world

I soar upon higher realms
empowered in freedom's reign
mystic mysteries found
secret knowledge uncontained

Within divinity's light, I crest
filtering ancient teachings
to travel a path of spirituality
that few seem to be reaching

Awakened by impending dawn
glimpsing the talisman of my mind
I rise to met the world once more
saddened by the reality of mankind

Phylogenetic Relation
Written December 18, 2007

Limpid, he travels the corridors with felid movements,
a high powered being masquerading in human guise.
Once in awe, I stared deep into its transforming flesh,
living for the moments of resurrecting humanity.

Years pass as the lotus blossoms, cycling lifetimes
as though they were victims of Chinese water torture.
Affections growing to depths only known in dreams,
until manifestation overrides reality's tainted tethers.

Now starving, I linger for the presence of his splendor
to cascade gently over my being with cool shimmers.
Secure in the knowledge that he too, shall be saved
from implanted mind warps, infringing upon free will.

Sentinels wander aimlessly, forces to inhibit a union
long forged in decades of centuries come and gone.
Aggravated shame of peers, their weapon of choice
but divinity refuses to deny our hearts, again reborn.

Limpid, we travel the corridors with felid movements,
high powered beings masquerading in human guise.
Now in awe, peers stare deep into transformed flesh
waiting to witness the moment we resurrect humanity.

Working a Mystery

Written June 26th, 2002

As I walked in the room, I whispered
'you know the words, you know the ways'
as energies stirred, reminding me
long ago, I chose this path to take

They waited at the quarters, watching
as I gazed around this room I'd made
years had gone by since I painted the lines
these symbols, this circle of sacred space

It was like no time had passed at all
since I'd walked between the worlds
with ease and grace the elements came
and once again listened to my words

The gates were open, the circle closed
energies gathering above the cauldron
my hands weaving and voice intoned
to contain the energies I'd called in

Scents of Dragon's Blood and Myrrh
surrounding me in swirls of mist
enchantments brewing in my mind
words sung softly from my lips

Chanting down to the final moments
intentions focused, visualization keen
I knew this was the right moment
to let the power free to do it's thing

Releasing the energies into the night
for the manifestation to begin
I whisper "So Mote It Be"
as the spell flies away on the wind

The quarters released, the circle open
I stop for a moment to take it all in
the scent of the room, glow of the candles
finally I'm at peace with myself once again

Static Cling
Written July 8th, 2007

Aventurine cloaks encircle feminine wiles.
Apathetic grumbles meet adoration extreme.

Life Spark
Written May 30th, 2005

From darkened hallways, ivory beckons.
Pristine doorways, defying the gloom of life
Though shaken, I step with ease,
from threshold, to threshold, hovering.
Awaiting a sign, from the crossroads,
to speak to me of pathways and dangers

Hope eludes me for moments,
each door seemingly the same as the next.
The shrouded hands of waifs, reaching,
striving to pull me into their abyss.
Closing my eyes, I seek divine intervention
in answer, it comes...

Smooth, pale golden light, skimming my aura,
tapping as though it were a hand, cleansing me.
Willing me to look above the glowing doorways.
erasing my anxiety with serenity's waves.
Until softly, it opens my eyes in revelation,
as an ankh of ivory, slowly turns.

Blindly, in faith, I walk through the doorway.
The ankh appearing, in a spark against my throat,
surging with energies, as it quickens my soul.
Here in the creamy ivory clouds, of a narrow corridor,
I travel, no longer in fear, but with purpose
into the brilliance of another life, reborn

Healing Slumber
Written May 15th, 2006

Hidden, she slowly awakens veils of mystery, her shroud
Caught between the worlds of ones that only doubt

Streams of colors, denied within fabrications of love
Turned the reddest heart into a ashen pile of dust

Remember, dreams process, knowledge flowing endlessly
and there she finds familiarity in eyes of thunderous gleams

Solitary now in ancient ways, they watch, denial their truth
No, her power never left her it merely hid from life's abuse

Star Shudder
Written March 24th, 2005

In the enchantment of the moon's glow, as the wind begins to howl
voices can be heard of those we hold dear seeking to find our essence
in the starlight's mist

And as the mist carries the stardust to touch the shoulder that we seek,
both souls shudder in unison, for they know they have been touched
by the beauty of a heart's light

So I ask you,
have you shuddered beneath the stars this night?

Hinged Reality
Written July 21st, 2007

Carousel, an illusion of time
thwarted by effortless whims;
confine denial's maze

Lone pathways do serve
willing dreams for realists
as they starve affectionately.

Destiny has arrived. Have you?

Reclamation
Written July 23rd, 2005

Blazes of light surround my face as if I'm walking in a dream
Through realms unknown, uninhibited at breakneck speed

Free from my body, flooded in light I drift through pieces of my life
finding all the things that matter are still within my sight

The chaos and dread are gone, enthusiasm takes it's place
for I will once again fly and tonight I spread my wings

Through time and space I glide taking back what once was mine
you sought to destroy me and lost, from my sight, I suggest you hide

Journeyman
Written July 18th, 2007

Akasha awaits karmic crusades
Wicked enlightenment seeking initiates, touring vast extremes
Warps of time, reality in omnipresent waves
Transgressions recorded

Mind Masquerade
Written March 17th, 2006

How tragic it comes to play, shadowing mind, body and soul
without a trace of purpose to the victim it bestows

A lingering smoke façade, whims of games, hidden fancies
lurking like habits of beggars, lost in recesses of fantasy

Beyond life's mundane dirge, light races upon shadow's play
Paramount in its diversion, setting the phoenix to flames

Ablaze in elemental embrace flutes beckon golden hues
Inviting lost spirits to arise, healing's fantasia resumes

Psyches rejoice serenity, indigo spirals light the way
euphoric, empowered splendor, we dance in paths of gray

Separate beings, complete, no remorse to fill our hearts
confusion gone, memory intact, we part, respectful of our song

Karmic Venom
July 15th, 2007

Reptilian adventures,
carefully woven with double edged swords,
meet nostalgia.

Death's companion
for wasted youth.

Veiled
Written November 7th, 2005

Beneath the veil of my flesh lies secrets unexplored
beyond the diminishing abyss of a soul seemingly scorned

Hollow echoes of the past cling like star dusted hues
against a withered heart resurrected for you

Enchantments can't sustain the passion filling my soul
nor break the loneliness denying dreams I hold

Blinded, you linger with intentions unclear
I seek to reach your heart as you will me to disappear

Shadows seek to lure me once again to their embrace
but I was indigo and gold long before you came

Beyond lustful games, past society's screams
I'll emerge like the phoenix riding upon dragon's wings

Beneath the veil of my flesh will lie secrets unexplored
beyond the diminished abyss of a soul, once again reborn

Enslave Me (Tangerine) – An Acrostic Poem
Written July 15th, 2005

Tantalize me, won't you?
Asphyxiate me with your scent.
Nourish the primal lust,
Grinding beneath my innocence.
Explore uninhibited.
Reach into the core of my depths.
Internally invade me.
Nectars await in passion's grip.
Enslave me!

Kiss of Ra
Written May 12th, 2005

Cascading sands glow like powdered gold
beneath the brilliance of the mid-day sun
Warm breezes carrying it to mist my body
wrapping me within the embrace of Ra

Within sacred space I stand, eyes closed
my faced turned into his flowing rays of gold
Like a lover, awaiting the passion of his kiss
his heat stroking my face, feeding my soul

Sinking within the sands of gold, we meld
encircled within the loop of the sacred ankh
his heated kiss, stealing my breath in waves
cleansing my spirit, allowing rebirth to start

Quivering, I lie within the aftermath of his love
my aura shimmering like freshly polished gold
Empowered, my blessed spirit soars freely
watching Ra disappear within the sunset's folds

54

Divine Ecstasy
Written April 17th, 2005

Ice etchings on wicked sand, breathe like the hour glass of time
Wafting through debris, long cluttered within the hollows of the mind

Scrapping wounds, they bleed you as though polishing your flesh
Revealing layers kept hidden behind the faces of our masks

Visions flowing, emotions reeling, twisting your heart into tiny knots
Showing no mercy in releasing all the shadows you'd forgot

Euphoria claims your writhing body, such sweet death, this ecstasy
As golden waves fill you gently your spirit soars in mysteries

Cartouche
Written July 29th, 2007

Class has no bearing on solar antiquities
as they line marble slabs

Though emotions toil within glistening gemstones,
life's cycle moves on

Inevitably confirming the posh are peasants
when dust comes to call

Transfiguration
Written August 19th, 2007

Golden rays once graced me,
empowered beams, unleashed
exalted compliments reigned
though humility always peaked

Transgressions spoiled emotion
Sewage boils in hate contained
Havens lurked in skeletal closets
A fashion statement, freely made

Self forgotten, I blamed the kiwi
it's pubic skin and sweetened taste
regurgitating bile of love's corpse
filling my flesh as a witness, keen

Silhouettes arrived in milky quartz
ebony games of religious claims
distortion their weapon of choice
lucidity riding in elusive cascades

Duplicated, my spirit rebellious
manipulated its weakened state
vengeful, it claimed resurrection
against the egotistical crusades

Humility always peaks in glory
exalted compliments shall reign
empowered beams unleashed
I am indigo, golden embraced

Disenchantment
Written July 13th, 2007

Dormant passions
overlook whims of fantasy

Chinese water tortures
impeding spirit's growth

Until feathered affections
permeate emotional walls
with volcanic eruptions

Lust's aftermath rejoices
hollow victories
written in ashen despair

Excused Rebuttal
Written July 7th, 2007

Humanity really is pathetic.
A society in denial, whiners.
Self forgotten spirits in flesh

Destiny is blameless, its chosen.
Karma does not scorn, but teaches.

YOU create life, YOUR reality
Take your time, make it worthy.

Witches (Acrostic)
Written August 28th, 2005

Wise ones, entrance me
Intuition your solemn guide
Teaching ancient mysteries
Cast upon indigo skies
Harboring elemental forces
Escaping reality of time
Seduce me with your mind

Unrequited Love
Written October 28th, 2005

A rainbow's glow of silence
lost in a shadow's mask

The Longing
Written April 28th, 2002

Mystery's sands seethe,
like blackened mist on borrowed time.
As innuendos flow rampant,
hidden beneath the veil of mundane lives.

Naked
Written November 27, 2002

Fire roars on the darkest night. My soul burns as though it's the flames.
I stand before the Triple Goddess for the first time, filled with rage.

Lifting my head with gentle fingertips, her eyes look deep into my soul.
I hear her voice inside my head, as I tremble with emotion, uncontrolled.

"You hide within yourself trying to conceal your pain, be naked, let it out,
embrace me. Release the misery, be full of life once again"

Taking my hand we began to dance, almost sensually in the fire's light.
First came the anger in black rage as the thunder roared through the night.

Lightning struck the earth boldly, my fears finally shaken away.
She let me go and as I danced, light enveloped me in mysterious ways.

Insecurities floating away as I swirled, tears of blood stream from my eyes.
The light is beautiful and blinding as my body shakes and trembles inside.

Here I am standing before you, confusion blown away with the winds.
My defenses down, my anger gone, vulnerable, naked, heart wide open.

Gaze upon me now and see me. Look into my heart and soul.
Beyond the words, beyond the skin look inside, see me as I truly am.

Judge me not for what I've done or the careless words I've spoken.
Answer me one question true, am I the monster that made you broken?

Stale Shudders
Written August 4th, 2007

Sacrificial integrity
baits wounded hearts
like metal shards in heat

Toiling against
blistered flesh, irrelevant
to impassioned cries

There, sated enemies
find fascination lacking luster
in unions of vain attempts
to heal wounded pride

Slithering Perfection
Written August 2nd, 2007

Satire glances peak ridicule
an infestation of the subconscious
roaming through light waves
siphoning life forces

Negativities flail in self defense
collapsing assaulted auras
much like fireflies smeared
against sole-less shoes

And there in hollow victory
unity stands in denial
awaiting a self satisfaction
only found in toxic mirrors

Ashen Thunderstorms (Inlaid Acrostic)
June 16th, 2005

Calloused, ash scented fingertips,

Roam
  Elegantly
   Adoring
    Crimson
    Hues

   Pausing to

     Feather
     Over
     Remnants

    of faded lipstick

      Memorizing
      Ecstasy

As thunderstorms gaze into feline, charcoaled eyes questioning their
motives of desire.

Insecurities
   glimmer in tears,

     Leaking
     Obscure
     Visions
     Entrapped

    within the veils of a haunted heart

       Yielding
       Opaque
       Ubiquitous

        Silence

Azure Reign
Written September 25th, 2005

Supreme power resonates
faceless in reality
seen through eyes of all

Masked, personified
sublime serenity
answers our calls

One power, one source
named by a million tongues
guides the shifting tides

Encrypted in divinity's light
balanced perfection
claims androgynous rides

All seeing and knowing
belonging to no one
eluding mundane confines

The age of enlightenment
beckons to us all
reigning azure skies

Craft Survival *(Theban)*
Written July 10th, 2007

Survival's art validated
by the brilliance of vast misconceptions;
championed devout falsities with Runes of Honorius

Blood threads of like minds
instilling life's knowledge; discarded as scrolls of tatter.
Ancient secrets of the wise halting paganism's demise

Alchemic Fire
Written July 2nd, 2005

South ardor flows from dragon's breath
torches of which alchemist take heed
for by their request they've summoned
this quarter of ancient powers that be

Upon fervent flames they steadily gaze
chants working energies as they billow
fueling combustion within the element
kindling their properties ebb and flow

Guardians summoned await their need
within their temporal colored blaze
streaming orange, red and yellow hues
representing the angels they contain

Radueriel, Israfel, Shemiel and Uriel
along with Metatron bring their reign
as songs and dance consume the ritual
building the power they must maintain

Fire ascending with their primal forces
passion, courage, creativity and strength
proceed uninhibited to fill the pentacle
beyond the earthly realms of the mundane

In final release they rage the winds
combustion mirroring sunlight's rays
wielding intents of manifestations
universally ignited upon astral planes

Acknowledged for their presence
thanked respectfully for their power
with "blessed be" upon her sacred lips
the high priestess releases the quarter

Insuring catastrophe shall not occur
by leaving eternal fires to linger
for she knows they belong to no one
and would retaliate with great vigor

Opium Poppy *(Acrostic)*
Written July 30th, 2005

Obscured visions of ecstasy
Protrude holographic haze
Igniting mind fires of manifestation
Ubiquitous lucidity arising triumphant
Mesmerizing even fantasia of the mind

Pestilence arrives, sickle in hand
Oblivious to conscious hysteria
Peeking through waves bloody coughs
Permanently cementing an addiction
Yearning only for death's embrace

Cameo
Written May 17th, 2004

His mother's face haunted his thoughts
as he slowly carved the onyx by hand.
Her delicate silhouette becoming immortal
within a timeless trinket of memories,
to be worn about his daughters neck

Drifting
Written February 17^t, 2007

Drifting into nothing, grabbed by hands unseen
my body jerks as mind screams
but my lips smile awaiting the ecstasy
that hides in the essence of the unknown

Crescendo
Written February 15th, 2007

It's bittersweet really, your touch
cascading down my back invitingly
lingering at the nape of my neck
musky scents teasing the senses
leaving ghost trails of happiness

I wonder how often it's suited you
on whims of fancy, boyish charms
surfacing through an aged mind
promising illusions of lustful youth
yielding seed to barren hollows

Sublime frenzied fantasy, untamed
reckless as it travels light waves
deluded acts, justifying false hopes
in those feeling beyond the mundane
with hopes of love fulfilling lonely lives

When tears fall against swollen flesh
striving to sever insanity's mind game
and desperate hands seek warmth
will you be the savior forging a reality
or laughter echoing tattered souls

Dead Space
Written February 18th, 2007

Vagrant voices churn
foul mouthed, disrespect
seemingly fair game
breeding contempt

Awaiting the silence
I move to cease the day
fate disconnects
and chatter fades

Indigo Dreams
Written on February 22, 2007

Solidify my tainted woes with your heart's caress
Stifling fears as I nestle against your warm chest
Voice words only heard in the hopes of the mind
As together we ascend beyond space and time

Climb with me through the ethers, fully entwined
Beyond those that tend to judge with prying eyes
As we empower each other within serenity's keep
Lovers claiming their hearts upon indigo dreams

Fox Notion, Powerful Potion (Fox Medicine)
Written February 24th, 2007

Walking crystalline
A woven camouflage, deadly
Igniting cosmic forces, supreme
A lonely apathy for the mundane
Exchanging mute glances

Between the worlds I walk and speak

Popularity discarded, denied
Self preservation in society's disdain
Transcending surrounding chaos
A stealthy time bomb, ticking
Omni-potent, Omni-Present

An enchanted keeper of invisibility

My reality, power extreme
Un-exhibited to those unenlightened
Cunning, sensing all and knowing
Seemingly shunned by passer bys
A veiled deception, waiting to rise

Plainly in sight, though rarely seen

Hunted by the enlightened
Misunderstood fiery energies toil
Convicted by ignorance, tortured by life
Reaching balance amidst clouded emotions
Snickering solemnly in the sidelines

Sensual allure, an asset, banefully perceived

Warrior, predator, silently keen
Warping in a vortex of humane healing
Enraptured your spirits greedily reach
For scraps of my essence
But you can never tame me

My den secure in failed conceptions of me

Purgatory
Written July 20th, 2003

Shards of glass, my aura makes
as remnants of my heart explode
Visions filter through my mind
a love for which my soul was sold

Maggots permeate my tongue
eating away the mouth you kissed
Blood seeping from every pore
as I'm rejected by the abyss

Doomed to stare in utter daze
at the life that I have missed
Chained in torture on the edge
without release of death's bliss

Acid tears flow from the eyes
that were once adored
My womb cries for the fetus lost
when you proclaimed me whore

Dayglow's Aftertaste
Written April 28th, 2007

Passion's heat, merely an anvil
of destruction's waiting hollow
forces denial from tear ducts

As stained redemption reeks sour dreams
mingled in sheets of love wishes
denied morning breath
in the silence of sun beams

Night Eagle (Owl Medicine)
Written March 5th, 2007

Silence yields the fearless and wise
From the east, breathing magic to life
Upon balance of shadows and light
Illumination's Night Eagle takes flight

Deceiver feathers lay in their wake
Evidence that they've slain their prey
Some natives fear this sign of death
Others see symbols of nature's breath

Shamans, sorcerers and witches alike
Walk with this medicine by their side
Traveling their paths, crossroads await
Where dark arts tempt the hands of fate

Be wary, for betrayal talons will seize
Shape-shifters arise, sealing destiny
Heed the warning of omniscient eyes
And they shall yield spiritual allies

Great seekers of truth traveling dreams
To bestow gifts of ancient mysteries
Seeing through deceptions with ease
Mind whispers, their enlightened keys

Through their power, courage will come
To face the darkness, make it your own
For spiritual release to sacred domains
Embracing the light upon astral planes

69

Poltergeist Effect
Written on March 18th, 2007

Hallowed silence haunts
where tears reign, self inflicted
A true release of preservation
yielding manifested lovers
Born of lonely hearts
and broken soul's refuge

Phantoms collide
on a quest for happiness
Denying the inevitable
with blatant disregard to life
Loyalty shattered in a moment
for a shred of unconditional love

Fate does readily exist
for the spiritually enlightened
Caught in the frenzy of society
healing humanity with little thanks
They suffer a dismal reality
exile from those holding their hearts

Consciousness splitting
until fragments of the mind seek
par excellence upon spiritual realms
Deemed sinister on earthly planes
as their mundane needs are fulfilled
by empowered miracles

Misconceptions of the norm
shun these beings, the purest hearts
Creating the illusion of insanity
forcing survival at all cost
While the cure for ghostly obsessions
is simply the human touch

Jagged
Written July 29th, 2007

Severed euphoria,
chalkboard nails

Cryptic solace contained
within banshee's wails

Sunberry Bride
Written April 8th, 2007

Passions conjure cravings,
Delectable consummated with innocent taste buds
Brewing sublime seedlings within facets of the mind

Wanton fingers embrace Sunberry stems, fondly
Wicked hand-me-downs of nature's hidden follies
bluntly tantalizing whims

Cherubs nestle too closely,
singing soft enchantments over pure spite brewed tea
Daring an eternal meshing of the most forbidden fruit

Resisting urges I breathe, fully expanding my lungs,
anticipation taking its hold, exploding into hot fantasies
steeping boldly in porcelain

Cerebral hemorrhage stings
My free will, merely a memoir, a lie upon fancy invitations
promising new beginnings as I embark upon demise

Emotional Sushi
Written June 28th, 2007

Rabid, they feast
Subconscious vamps
Weaving torment's siphons
Upon gilded dreams

Denial, their ally
Against Innocence raped
In destiny's hollow

Self Preservation's Twins
Written April 8th, 2007

Desperate they cling,
remnants of childhood so devilishly charming
lurking in dark hollows, hidden away from life

Often I've glimpsed them,
mirrors of my dreams, taunts of broken hearts,
wallflowers of youth refusing to fade away

Embracing my twins,
two for every trauma, I seek to release them,
willing them to break, to flee or waste away

Their laughter breaches
every wall I can fathom torturing threads of sanity
They walk silently defiant seeking to destroy you

Sweet Sister
Written May 2003

Sweet sister wont you sing
the song you left inside my soul
on a grassy knoll in Tennessee
where free, we used to roam

High atop the mountain
where the canyon meets the creek
near the shack they say is haunted
and the fireflies run deep

Skirts whirling in the moonlight
moonshine heavy on our breath
we danced around the camp fire
and told stories until we slept

I search for you now as I stare
upon the heavens in the sky
and will my soul to reach for you
as the tears fall from my eyes

You left me stranded in a memory
I can't clear from my head
echoing like church bells
carried upon the raging winds

I never got to tell you
the truest secret in my heart
I always wished to be like you
upon every falling star

Sweet sister wont you sing
the song you left inside my soul
into my ear, so I know I'm safe
upon my lonely journey home

Cradled Perfection
Written June 29th, 2007

Whiskers feather flesh
as heart beats unite

Souls completely in tune
Euphoria lost in time

Wasting Away
Written April 28th, 2005

Shadows linger on a life
where once the future shone
tossed away by insecurities
hidden away within your home

Devastated by the reality
of what you've come to be
wallowing in your fears
and self inflicted misery

You sought a life of freedom
yet turned down every chance
hating your own comfort zone
and side stepping romance

You let the days pass by you
never looking at the sun
then sit and wonder why it is
that your mind has come undone

Sacred Text
Written June 29th, 2007

Lapis silhouettes
breathe papyrus etchings
Mystery's keys
upon nature's foreskin

Panoramic Abstract
Written April 29th, 2007

Burnished charms beseech validity
Nestled between communion rails
Immune to their violated sanctity
Faith swallows redemptions will

Their lambency justified only with
Thoughts of beeswax illumination
Stroking breath of Christ's Blood
A vain attempt to purge the soul

Stellar warriors witness blasphemy
Defiling the verity of ancient ways
Kissed rings, their sigil of promise
of resurrection within pearly gates

A devout crusade to cast asunder
Demonic etchings of simple minds
Sanguineous flickers silence screams
Choired voices, sweet victory cries

Misplaced in the falsities of men
I ascend, watching it proclaimed
Satan's mistress purged of sin
My holy essence, Divinity's stain

Sanctity's Inquisitor
Written May 3rd, 2007

Blinding all innocence,
spores of lost realities softy choke humanity
in lavender hues and rose colored glasses
Taunting the misguided

As veiled misconceptions
yield pristine personas dating tiger lilies while
revamped happy endings starve on polished whims
and plastic attributes

What a lofty recourse
of positive thinking, churning in the daft minds of idiots
Slowly trickling conjurations of death within hypothermic
tears from laughing fools

Stained, we watch livid
beyond worlds, above faith, wondering where salvation lies
Knowing below the chaos once thrived a sanctuary
too exquisite for human life

Vacant
Written May 9th, 2007

Dormant, it beguiled, entrancing visitors
Sapphires on spirals, white smoke parading
through hidden camps forging into desires

Heart tremors seeking rebirth's vital right
beating to a harmony sought only in dreams
craving new beginnings a past life complete

Enchanted with a smile dissolved against glass
stained, hope withers red's green and gold
mute against diamonds turning slowly to ash

Modern Chimera
Written June 29th, 2007

Flippant transgressions,
permeate the senses.

White noise in blue jeans.

Smokey Night Songs
Written May 21st, 2007

Borderline infatuations spark simple hand gestures
Conjuring caressed images rising at the small of my back
The serpent swaying the mind

Small sparks of combustion
Empowering rhythmic tones undulate cravings of affection
Escalating primal instincts through desires untapped

Music drowns to muted tones, closing distance of heated fabric
Fusing hips, steady emotion between soft lip's cruel intentions
Heart beats lost in a charade

Dimmed lights take the promise
Stiletto clicks, a taunting echo of sweaty palms parting ways
Lonely pours from sour whiskey
Scratchy records sound the same

Meditation's Peak
Written June 30th, 2007

Within the folds of the lotus
Majestic inclines savor mysteries

Sounds of Numb
Written June 30th, 2007

Serenades inhibit transients unchained
reality...
a juke box of denial

Stained Perfection
Written May 22nd, 2007

Etched they stain me, lingering third eye lovers
devout, forbidden souls unintentionally conjured
Society's mismatch within a spiritual haven

The perfect balance accented warrior to womb
Eternally stretched in life amongst spirals of heaven
Blissfully passionate as one vibrant within each other

Grounded, agony remains wasting existence to please
badgering masses, unyielding, intent only on feeding frenzies
Life vamps instilling promises selfishly destroyed in vain

I will them away, him away, seeking refuge in isolation
Praying, setting him free, but closing my eyes, reality peaks
My heart is his, his hand is mine, lingering lovers entwined

Stagnant Guardian
Written May 22nd, 2007

It echoes poison innuendos.
Milestones of youth's debris
knocking the faint of heart with spasmodic overtures.

Disgusted, heavens weigh.
Mimics of chatter torture my existence, in plain view.
A recognition of power plays

Often I've wandered, silently
Glimpsing God-like personas, toying with lives.
Shattering brothers on whims of vanity

Upon crossroad's branches I await unity.
Solemnly choking on bile of unreleased saline.
Waiting for sanity to fuse

Vertigo
Written June 30th, 2007

Delayed motion,
such a timeless enchantment

Nirvana's escape from the
potentially sound
to everlasting mortality

Television
Written June 30th, 2007

Humanity's humor teaches nothing.
Only open minds bring mysteries.
Discipline Required

Metamorphosis
Written June 29th, 2007

Graced perfection within nature's arms
Entwine feline accents of soul

Courtesan
Written May 27th, 2007

Slow suffocation has eluded me
Dreams of family come and gone
Fanciful frenzy a secret doorway
My claim to fame, lustful songs

Ensnared, they succumb divinely
to flawless skin and silken thighs
Painted lips frolicking innuendos
Sordid games excite bored lives

Sins ease in moments of nirvana
Mirrored reflections, stolen time
Lavender mingled with rich musk
Happiness chilled in tainted wine

Scorned yet pampered, I do survive
A lethal thorn within society's court
Beautifully confident, silently amused
A primed vixen awaiting her consort

Amethyst Dreams
Written June 30th, 2007

Third eye beams captivate the mundane

Reality's sense shock,
an adaptation of power seething the soul

Blind ambition, amethyst awaits

Antiquated Originality
Written July 1st, 2007

Feigned smiles whisper invitations as mockery abounds

Gatekeepers erect, white noise intrudes
Defenses steady, group antics disrupted
Silence follows social annihilation

Witch tears equal destruction

School Yard
Written July 3rd, 2007

Anxiety, paper planed

"He Loves Me"

Sated juvenile hunger

Extinction
Written July 1st, 2007

Psychedelia seeks secrets of Nirvana
wasting resources of human nature

Epiphany arrives channeled
Dis-ease resolved

Universal Spawn
Written July 3rd, 2007

Vulgarity's orb meets quintessence
Divinity's breath

Windershin spirals purge violations conquering decay
Deosil, the adept masters animation

Rebirth presents... Earth

Tethered
Written on July 5th, 2007

Feelings abused, she gazes at stardust
knowing whiskered kisses await

Gumshoe
Written June 30th, 2007

Antiqued ethics weep mosaic tar
Nike molded to perfection

Morality's answer to rat infested streets

Gumshoe Observations (Expanded version of "Gumshoe")
Written on July 3rd, 2007

Splintered wood taunts my elbows as
Antiqued ethics meet cobblestone graffiti
Society's disdain upon upstanding citizens
Seeking solitude in once pristine grounds

Sensitivity shunned, brash youths reign reptilian
Answering the homeless with rat infested streets
While capitalizing materialism with hollow victories

Weeping mosaic tar, Nike molded to perfection
Downtrodden masses despise pre-mummification
Slowly ascending to anarchy, self-preservation

Enlightenment's age is upon us in splendor
White noise echoing the violation of humanity
In vigorous shifts, we move consciousness

Karma demands restitution of shallow patrons
Workers of Light, seek foul breathed souls
The napkin conscience de-wormed by necessity

Acceptance distilled, inhabitants move freely
Olden ways resurrected as ancestors applaud
Seeds of kindness dissolve internal dis-ease
I watch in awe, inhaling serenity's finality

Stalemate
Written on July 3rd, 2007

Crippled by cellophane
Cumulus nimbus halts at impervious sphere

Negativity Dissipates
leaving effervescent cascades

Dissection thwarted
Violated sanctity rejuvenates cells

Tea Tree Shower Hazard
Written on July 4th, 2007

Baneful droplets unleashed
upon cheeky caverns

Sensual sensations meet catastrophe

Sacred Slumber
Written on July 4th, 2007

Upon lotus petals we ascend

An ageless pillow of affection
beckoning past lives to bear eternity

Musky scents linger, divine

Halted Perception
Written on July 5th, 2007

Indigo charmed, balance is foretold

Cherub meshed, feminine wiles
meet masculine charms with silver cords

Lovers teased by fate's union

Lone Tremor
Written on July 6th, 2007

Streamlined,
motion pictures ebb against indigo

Eradicated hope plagiarizing dreams
of fulfilled hearts

Credit denial

Eagle Eye Justice
Written on July 6th 2007

Denial's catalyst
of pristine mannerisms
in impromptu settings

A bewilderment,
falsity reigns
with righteous indignation

Blasé
Written on July 6th, 2007

Chilled disdain seeks subliminal thoughts
replacing affections with contempt

~Acceptance~

Bittersweet after-bites of passion's core

Internal Toxicity
Written on July 7th, 2007

Opportunities vanish in sedated emotion,
conjuring self contempt

Life's pawn of jest
in close minded facets

Self love, our soul food,
wasted in envy's wake

Twin Serpents Arise
Written on July 7th, 2007

Lucidity, an aggravated assault

Stained glass windows of over-affectionate spirits
healing physical bodies with rape construed scenes

Enlightened senses tortured with release
Separation denied

Lily Pads
Written on July 7th, 2007

Stiletto tongues absorb poison swiftly
a toxic domination of wall flowers

Retribution...

Flies dawdle willingly in regurgitation
only to suffocate between frog lips

Flowers bloom

Shallow Inhabitants
Written on July 8th, 2007

Rigid elegance dominates society,
prompting false ethics with monetary gain

Masquerading penguins tethering Irish roses
A tainted dance un-squarely obtained

Life Support
Written on July 8th, 2007

Bosoms are charisma,
paramount in gentile minds.

Manifesting whores of ladies
with velveteen flutters
and two dollar shoes.

Mint prestige overshadows
such mildewed fascinations.

Euphoric qualities
caressing impoverished threads.

As manifestation beckons,
mind wars for heart songs
rise beneath blood moon wisps

Revealing a sanctity
only found within rugged limbs.

Leviathan
Written on July 8th, 2007

Horror stricken
entrails seek divine intervention
A willing adaptation
taming society's deeds

Overtures coronate
panic disorders to reign
webbed personas of reality
upon dreamscape scenes

Ice Cream in Chains
Written on July 8th, 2007

Surface postures, confident in cellophane
plummet to fragility

Midlife regrets
etching tourmaline in menses' cavern

Hardcore personas
can't rectify omissions

Futures bleak
without children's laughter

Illuminated Gusts *(Haiku)*
Written on July 8th, 2007

Beckoning Twilight
Jasmine drifts effortlessly
Whispers of the moon

Bitter Sour Remedy
Written on July 8th, 2007

Psychological hair antiquated against cedar
Liquid fire memories home delivered

Euphoria's Anecdote
Written on July 8th, 2007

Memoirs of bliss
repeat excessively

Cloaks of fascination
shielding torture from hollow skin

Mirrors squeal
distrust with venom

Contusions equate
logic's anecdote

Wake up! Survive!

Liquid Amber
Written on July 8th, 2007

Silken cheeks savor sweet fantasies
Nectars too sordid for retribution

Metamorphosis
Written June 29th, 2007

Graced perfection within nature's arms
Entwine feline accents of soul

Spirit Hearts
Written on July 10th, 2007

We stand united spirit to spirit, humans denying society's inhibitions
Captivated essences with a bond few want or care to understand
Our victories forged as one sex, unashamed
Entwined as lovers we faced you all head on with pride.

Alive!

Combustion (Love Ritual) - Acrostic
Written on July 10th, 2007

Calloused fingertips roam elegantly
Over contours of silken flesh
Memorizing each response as they
Boldly await internal fires to rise as
Ubiquitous passions permeating the
Senses in waves of heightened euphoria.
The aftermath of lover's hearts
Inviting primal urges to ascend into
Overtures contained only within
Nirvana's sacred grasp

Irreconcilable differences
Written on July 12th, 2007

Toxicity demands attention, violating personal space;
controlling measures for shallow minds and wounded hearts.
Avoid the stagnation, separation is imminent.

Mind Hearted
Written on July 13th, 2007

Nature fornicates elusions of perfection.
A tepid dance of waste trapped in society's wake.

Perceptions of life mates abound with severity;
crushed hearts seeking faults within self limitations.

Reality, feminine wiles tip scale's in grave proportions.
We are loneliness, starved.

Life's Retrospect
Written July 13th, 2007

Soul mates grieve within silver bands, un-matching.
Destiny, un-realized gone to waste.
Honesty was mistaken.

Stained Reality
Written July 13th, 2007

Emotions have no bearing on cyanide effects.
Death is inevitable.

X-tasy
Written on July 13th, 2007

Eradicated senses peak divinely with sordid hallucinations.
Blow me up.

Moldy Stones Weep
Written July 13th, 2007

Grass strokes macabre etchings
staining empathy with nature's breath.

A willful tease of oats against brittle bones;
threatening to rise as rebirth's temptress.

Banshees wail for less in afterlife and yet to us,
the grave is merely a commonplace, dismissed.

Bloodlines
Written July 13th, 2007

Meditated realities conjure comforts in midlife crisis
Ancestors arrive soothing my unused womb affectionately

Sorrow's acceptance

Tears to diamonds, my legacy survives
Hidden in depths of my brother's children's eyes

Scampi
Written July 15th, 2007

Saline buildup inhibits joy's reality.
Beckoning the wary with promises of flavored savoring
Stench cultivates regurgitation reflexes.
Another bad date.

Glistening
Written June 30th, 2007

Euphoric drops caressing warm flesh
Love's perfection in nature's mist

Old Fashioned Embrace
Written July 14, 2007

By fire's silence, I await flannelled memories to pass,
Sated against foundations forged by love's steady hand
Bing's crooning vinyl rounds, setting tempos to cascades
Hart's sorrow leaking saline, a dance for one left to decay

Christmas spice permeates, lights teasing popcorn chains
its specialty lacking warmth since he passed pearly gates
Whispers paint his portrait, sibling eyes conjure strength
restricting snow to outdoors we strive to save the holiday

She arrives emanating light, an Irish angel, emerald eyed
striving for our sakes alone to keep a family full of life
Beneath trims, gifts await bearing both their names
resurrection of her stability allowing marriage to remain

Fascination
Written June 17, 2003

Fascination reigns in a mind that wakes
A sleeping mind is stagnant and decays

Would you dare to open your mind
or will you simply let it waste away?

94

Caravan of Life (Gypsy Welcome)
Written July 14, 2007

Alive, we are rhythm, nature's extreme
begotten of forgotten, prestigious centuries

Lite's preservers on heritage we thrive
stifled by man's law, traveling to survive

Glide with us, united beneath forgotten dreams
singing valor songs and historical deeds

Olden way encased rubies of internal fire
a family strengthened by cultural desires

Saline Antics
Written July 14, 2007

Milky seams tether mind warps, tortures of extremes
Fate's jesters binding crossroads, life's jagged dreams

Lucidity's shadow moves to fade, cherished victories
Clock alarms, my savior against the depths of me

Elusive Thoughts
Written July 15th, 2007

Succulent thoughts waste in melodramatic trauma;
centralizing energy vamps in close encounters.

Unleashed, psychic chants eradicate emotions;
defenses cultivated against feigned invitations of creative endeavors.

Solitary confinement breeds brilliant extremes.

Saturn Lies
Written July 30th, 2007

Wielding concentric rings
a universal prisms awaits
mind bending reality

Translucent Affections
Written July 15, 2007

Eye falsities bear not my soul, unequipped in flesh and bone
though tenderized anatomy welcomes desires coursed

Intrepid wills, logic depraved, spy beyond human walls
upon sterling chains, lucidity captivates my foreign form

Entwined consorts, surviving far beyond humanity's thorns

Creative Integrity
Written July 16, 2007

Lapis Convictions never bow
to envious stems of calla lily streams

A handicapped game
for mischievous wiles hidden in gossip whores

Trite anticipation
merely fuels dictated crossroads soiling regal intentions

Stardust breathes only positive traits,
creativity held within passion's reign

Mirrored Delight
Written June 30, 2007

Feminine wiles soothing heartbeats
against the solidity of earth shoes

Draconic Whims
Written July 21, 2007

Realms forsaken in heart whispers
quake muted tones, healing vibrations
lost in fantasy's tale of reality, false eyes
glimpse decorative hues, unknowingly

Earth's gatekeepers glide majestic
bearing humanity's burdens, silent
warriors consuming negativity's beat
as we move as drones through life

Elemental fire, wavers delightfully
at childish fascination, riding dreams
of winged inhabitants, light saviors
teaching ancient ways, to us alone

Shallow Clusters
Written July 26, 2007

It blisters my cheeks trickling spasms of affection
against forlorn skin, without mercy of tidal waves
Though I do prefer it to searing blood vessels; reflecting
I ponder this venom of nature reckoning temptation's fate

How evolution sold me enslaved to Coppertone's rays
reviving hopeful blushes against slow burned demise
Lessons, always lessons, yet teaching nothing but loss
A grand hurricane echoing past lives in dreamer's lies

Reclusive hearts, do yearn adventures of skinny dipping
traveling dangerous currents of freedom's wake
Too bad shark infestation breeds rocky shores, not life preservers
Happiness was a peace maker lost in sunset's embrace

Wrinkled Memoirs
Written August 1st, 2007

Though moist sheets witness primal rites
devouring loneliness in spasmodic dismay
Burgundy fascinations never entertained me
the way school boy charms struck fancies

Masterfully disguised in mischievous armor
forlorn anticipations slenderize inhibitions
Until thighs too smooth seek depths unknown
whispering promises maturity soon ignores

Of course zesty images do keep in stained glass
but mahogany notches never outlast termites
Debris retains evidence fondling down pillows
and masquerades end when bottles run dry

Wall Paper

Written June 30th, 2007

Repetitive, it glares ashamed to be seen
amidst severed ties of broken dreams

Devoid of emotion, solid colored to fade
lost, antiquated, awaiting new days

Bridged Transgressions

Written August 5th, 2007

Stalemate should never be suited
Life's a game that's not win or lose
Drawing from the realms of reality
too often discarded in dismal issues

Crossroads beckon from towers
emotions churning reactive minds
And there within the chaos, we die
seeking rebirth within spiritual tides

We cross bridges of enlightenment
unsure to steady steps, we roam
No longer shaken by society's noise
braced in self empowerment's hold

Here we claim our fame, our soul
accepting faults, quite free of blame
Assured of our paths in this lifetime
we dive to earth to spend our days

Knowing happiness never eluded us
we just cast it aside, a fearful game
Now we only hear it's laughter echo
against jaded shells of the mundane

True Lives
Written July 1, 2007

Society's bane,
merely destiny's illusion
escaping soul food

Quaint, pristine
coddled insecurity
obstacles displaced

Personification
is our reality
quite enchanted

Life's Aftertaste
Written September 11, 2004

Warrior to servant, ridden beyond death's path
gazing into the memories of a black looking glass
through lifetimes of triumphs and hollow victories
running naked beneath the moon's crying beams

Gazing through the fortress of a lost soul's demise
gripping bones exposed, hunger torturing the mind
euphoric glimpses of love's scents once inhaled
overshadowed by corpses, that once I'd impaled

Sorrow forsaken, amuck in the ego's grasp
taunting the lies of sinners, accepting life's aftermath
lost, alone yet sublime within the taint of misery
tasting thine own blood, that only now becomes sweet

Sorcery
Written June 30, 2007

Esoteric enigmas, cedar contained
forge a sanctity bound by blood

Hidden Lover's Dance
Written September 16, 2004

Firelight spawns visions against the dying sun
cresting like ember waves across the skyline
as the amber of the sky gives way to the moon
majestic in presenting its glimpse of twilight

With face upturned, softly smiling I wait
for the divine heated kiss of Amun Ra
as he gracefully makes way for Amunet
to embrace me within a protective shroud

Silvery shadows move against the winds
following as though trapped by my aura
spreading energies through each limb
as I dance to the tune of sweet euphoria

Iridescent eyes mingle against the hues
of earthen shapes, caressing autumn leaves
listening intently, upon sung chants they form
swirling enchantments, manifesting dreams

Soaring as one, cloaked in velveteen night
beyond mundane worlds, through etheric mist
mysteries, traveling uninhibited through time
as the hidden one awaits the return of his kiss

Pausing in a Moment's Dream
Written September 27, 2004

On the eve of morrows waking glance
stumbling into infinity I see
chaste ladies dancing fancy
upon a mid-summer night's dream

Gowns flowing in the wind
as though they were angel's wings
caressing the air in which they're spun
the purest of lovers in heavenly streams

What enchantments they weave
upon the sorrow of a lonely heart
whispering songs from smiling lips
as the rest of the world comes undone

Tainted by the lies of life
I long to touch their innocence once more
reminiscing of times of blissful youth
and the fine gown of splendor, I never wore

On dragon's wings, I've always gone to fly
chasing moon beams across a starlit sky
enjoying the touch of lovers, come and gone
left alone in the aftermath of broken hearted songs

I wish not to turn back the clock
Though I dream of the ladies, fair and sweet
their love and dancing in the mundane world
has never been enough to set me free

Ambrosia
Written July 1ˢᵗ, 2007

Lover's nectar
instilled within senses
infuse passions

Beckoning home
two destined bodies
Rituals begin anew

Akashic High of Etheric Flight
Written September 29, 2004

Stirring within the solace of sacred space
visions billowing through unseen winds
they come, speaking in different tongues
answering my call, beckoning me near
whispering enchantments in my mind

Swimming in a sea of fantasia's dream
on the velveteen blackness of the sky
descending from silvery moon beams
touching, taunting, reeling me in
quickening my senses to new heights

Akashic euphoria claiming the mundane
swirling away all that blocks it's way
swallowing it whole, in a flicker of pain
an ecstasy unmatched by cardinal sin
the ways of the witch, claim me once again

Mother Moon
Written June 30, 2007

Feminine power
awaits shy smiles
a lighted path to serenity

Nurturing spirals
commence healing

Enter Nirvana
its essence is free

Shattered Stalemate
Written October 3, 2004

I'm not inspired by your words of woe
nor the toxic tears of your ashen eyes
pouring pity upon a silken face
lived without remorse upon mankind

Your chaos is your own, not mine
seething through your every pore
shadowed only by the arrogance
that you are the master of us all

Splinters of your sadistic deeds
sent upon my aura shall not take
for the mirror returned it unto thee
my will is my own, not yours to take

I shall be golden, among the indigo
soaring above it all, live and free
while you fall from the throne of bones
left beneath your religion's withering tree

Akasha's Rain
Written October 26, 2004

Muted tones express thoughts not said
on a breeze of dawn that is yet to come
chilling my flesh in the heat of the night

Beckoning me solemnly beyond the veil
indigo mist dances before my sultry eyes
revealing that which is hidden to my mind

My limbs carry no weight as they sway
a trance through journeys traveled before
ancient seekers speak truths of long ago

Dazing euphoria grips my heightened senses
nature's drug to the enlightenment of the soul
forcing me to kneel against the earth's lush soil

Sweet ecstasy comes through waves of pain
as though a virgin feeling the heat of penetration
I crave more, though I feel I'm splitting apart

To lucid dreams I surrender as my body falls
peaceful at a glance, though the turmoil reigns
upon waking in the mundane world where I dwell
alive with the quickening of Akasha in my veins

Chandeliers Chime
Written on July 8th, 2007

Austrian crystals masturbate illusion
Frenzied climax deterred by reality's gaze

Dying within Autumn Winds
Written October 26, 2004

Brisk air fills my lungs, like shards of ice
leaving a pain much like the one of my heart
as the coolness of your tombstone
braces my back against the autumn winds

Upon the barren earth, ancient trees bleed
multi-colored leaves of life's essence withering
as though they were memories of our life
flowing to join in the dance of the dead

Though denial still fills my weary mind
part of me wishes to meld within them
and be whisked beyond the loneliness
into the hibernation of winter to come

I will your spirit to reach for me in comfort
as the sun breaks the clouds in defiance
striving to warm me against the bitter chill
though too late to save me from life's frost

For my soul, much like the gray of the stones
lacks the luster of the hues nature displays
for it wishes only for this body to wilt and die
releasing it once again, to soar away with you

Forest Guardian

Written November 6, 2004

I lie in wait as the winds come softly
threatening to chill my weary bones
silently against the tallest oak
willing it's essence to keep me warm

Beneath my feet energies stir
invoking the power of spirit within
as my earthly body leaves it's shell
I meld with the oak as winter begins

Centuries of ancient knowledge fill me
as I slumber and the year wheel turns
I feed the life source of the old oak
and it quickens my spirit in return

The forest shall await the spring
and I shall guard it with my soul
keeping watch inside the mother
the ancient, wise and fertile oak

Upon rebirth I continue my vow
to guard the forest from man's ways
gliding on wings, locked in a memory
of a past lifetime that clings each day

Vinyl Expectations
Written July 1st, 2007

Midnight tolls strange companions
Thumps run steady in the night

Stagnant rains, compelling heat
Spilling forth from apple wine

Tongues roll slightly, friendly banter
Such unnecessary woes

Frenzied limbs, seeking fantasy
in places they're unknown

Tower of Light
Written July 29, 2005

Nameless, faceless, timeless
Beyond a shadow's gate
Whispering words of surrender
Designed to seal our fate

Promising, threatening, watching
Beckoning on emotion's play
Willing the unknowing fool
To befriend darkness's rage

Enlightened eyes see through you
Too wise to rush and claim your task
Free will sets free the light you taint
Protected by the loyal Dragon's wrath

Here there are no demons or darkness
No belief of your Devil or your ways
Mind plays dissolved, you are powerless
For I am the divine light of sacred space

Keepsake's Box
Written July 1, 2007

Preservation
gilded on mahogany
serves sanity well
on sorrow's day

Denied Lust
Written June 30, 2007

Crimson lips
ignite flesh in release

Opaque glaciers
harbor resentment

Psychosis
Written June 30, 2007

Shocked nerves
Muscles tense
Serenity distorted
Enter mind's edge

Silver tongued
satin edged lies
perfection
moving pictures
echo severed ties

Unbridled
Written June 30, 2007

Unforeseen
arises sweet destiny

Witchery
Stone encased
kissing sonic waves

Phantom Kiss
Written March 19, 2005

Shadows spin visions through indigo hues.
Forbidden love twirling fantasy,
vividly spun in silver blue

Heated lips upon an angel's face,
keeping the devil in the dimple of his chin,
softly and hungrily meld with mine
as though it's where they've always belonged.
Taking my breath, giving me life
his touch spreading passions
I thought to be long gone

Fingers caress places
where fires once were tamed
stirring the depths within my soul
disturbing my once sacred space
Taunting and teasing
until my body begs to be released
I feel him move between my thighs
his kiss deepening once more
as I arch to meet his frenzy
the heat of lust consumes me whole

Whiskey
Written June 30, 2007

False courage
collides with comfort

Inept solutions
Draining misery's mistake

Senses of Spiritual Attraction
Written March 28, 2005

Ice cream in chains is all I've become
seemingly powerless to your heated touch
the mind watching your visions dance
there's no refusal within my body to respond

Passion heats, as shudders come and juices flow
the glacier of my heart slowly dripping away
as my spirit reaches the ethers to grip yours
images flow from my mind, returning your lust

Waves of pleasure grip my senses
lost in the whirlwind of our souls intertwined
as my mind begins to scream no, I ignore it
knowing reality will set in among dawn's time

Morning comes in a wave of euphoria
the sheets still warm from your energy's heat
as the alarm clocks shrieks reality's chime
sadness slowly begins to take hold of me

I stand alone in the shower, feeling my body ache
as only the aftermath of love making can do
numb to the heat of the water, steam rising around me
softly crying, knowing that my flesh shall never touch you

Mistress Hemlock
Written March 30, 2005

Mistress Hemlock won't you save me
from the tightening grip of passion's dance
locked within the embrace of a phantom
whose flesh has never touched my bed

Would you cool the fire that seethes
threatening to consume my very soul
riveting my writhing body to the sheets
as his visions cause me to lose control

Mistress Hemlock as I place you sacred
under the pillow and left pocket of my pants
would you bind the chakra that torments me
saving me from the torturous days ahead

Would you keep me calm and collected all day
as his flesh taunts me silently as we walk
knowing his slender hands will never touch me
for it's his spirit and mind that tends to stalk

Mistress Hemlock won't you save me
should my quivering will begin to break
and promise me a hasty, painless demise
when I brew you up for a midnight drink

Letting me slip away quite silently
to rise beyond the moon for eternal sleep
for my love grows along with my sadness
and I shall not let my soul slip away from me

Powerfully Numb
Written April 3, 2005

Waves of pain seek shadows
against my soft pale skin
where once silk caressed
and lovers stared in awe

Heat differs now, from then
signifying invisible lust
wielded as though with consent
upon a body lying dormant

Pleasure never seeps inside
though the body responds
denial screams in the mind
willing it all to end in peace

Sleep denies my weary frame
the mind traveling to memories
attractions that made me swoon
keeping sanity within chaos

Amun Ra peeks above the sky line
chasing the shadows to the night
bathed in gold, I rise empowered
my smile never reaching my eyes

Heart Surges
Written July 2007

Mesmerized by your beauty
I search enlightened sapphires
vulnerable to love's possibilities
Imagining whiskered caresses
against a cheek, forever lonely
hoping reality will never come

Suffocated
Written March 31, 2005

Now the passion's dead...

Beyond cemeteries of fantasy
wanderlust of happiness rains
dreams lost forever to the chill
of love's indignant embrace

Winds carry the moans of lust
and cries of wounded hearts
solidifying the sanctity of time
for tortured souls and harlots

Feathers fall upon snowy hills
as though bludgeoned by fate
leaving trails of liquid crimson
awaiting their shallow graves

Moonlight no longer comes
the sun long denied it's rays
for darkness heeds to nothing
once entering hallowed space

Suffocated by the heart's aftertaste

Astral Lovers

Written December 3, 2005

Rising through fallen glass
atop a seaside cliff
Daring eternity to light a fire
that never yearned to live

Balance bowed to euphoria
as masks of grandeur disintegrate
Naked and free, entwined
they travel universal wakes

Silver Shadows Fly

Written April 1, 2005

Something wicked your way comes
toils of turmoil shall now be done
spite relived on those that played
invading upon this sacred space

Those that sought to spy and pry
thought oblivious to enlightened eyes
know the truth if you can stand it
I watched it all and found it candid

Power seethes beneath silken mist
hid from all that sought its bliss
emerging within great tidal waves
ready to drown you in total rage

Look down no more upon my soul
in arrogance claiming me a whore
you know not the beast you've freed
when lighting the fire inside of me

Illusions of dreams cast asunder
twirling within a mundane blunder
that of which you thought naive
shall now make true fools of thee

Silent Watchers
Written April 5, 2005

Churning through the sands of time
we seek that in which you harbor
numbly watching for the moment
you seek to raise the cone of power

I see you all and I care not

Underestimated you have been
denied respect, we taint your will
but again you stand before us
a vision, free and empowered still

You have no power over me

What gifts have you that hide
beneath the smile on your face
or the shadows of your eyes
looking so brilliant, yet grayed

The mysteries are mine to keep

Hidden in the shadows we wait
knowing the time shall finally come
our patience grows thin, we're tired
and yet the silent fight goes on

Respect all and truth comes

What is it we can not fathom
this power that seethes inside
you are not one of us, we know
and it baffles our higher minds

Perhaps you look and do not see

Witch, tell us your inner secrets
do we watch endlessly in vain
perhaps we should just ask you
for you, have become our bane

Humility is a part of life, seek it

Stretching
Written April 9, 2005

Time caresses our wounds
pouring salt into the mix
of our blood and tears
weaving opaque claws
through portals of the mind
until we instill the desire
to break the chains

Freed, we reach out
past the shards of confusion
beyond self suffocation
shattering boisterous shadows
and misery's stalemate
into the light of ourselves
we fear the most

Rising upon divine euphoria
beyond the azure mist
where our feet never touch
the heated pavement
of that which was scorched
we soar, dancing to a tune
alive and all our own

Emotional Shutdown
Written October 27th, 2005

Battlements seethe the blood
lost on sorrow's tears
Shredding lines of light
denied the right to fear
For nothing is a choice
violations leave, all gone
To feel is nothing but a hole
of where the heart's already lost

Betrayal's Justice
Written April 17, 2005

Electric blue told the story
caught in a black spider's web
secrets kept an eternity
a sanctuary to the dead

Corpses seethed in anger
spirits arising from their dust
awaiting betrayal's justice
as the widow began to munch

Screams died upon the wind
wings left hanging all alone
stuck in a timeless dance
next to the fairy's little bones

The moon shone down in silence
calming the spirits once again
knowing the mysteries were kept
within the widows deadly den

And as the sun rose steadily
caressing the moon's starlight
both gave witness and declared
the keeper of secrets' great demise

An Afterthought's Smile
Written July 17, 2005

As I meld into the energies that transcend my soul
I ponder my greatest love and how it made me whole

Then questioning the sorrow and the pain it left me with
I realize without its' anchor, my spirit truly found pure bliss

Dormant Heartbeat
Written August 10, 2005

And I said to myself…

Random innuendoes of promiscuity founded in double standards
of the male species rarely result in emotions of love

Adding to the sobriety of loneliness of the female persuasion
ending in sexual gratification, lost in denial's crystalline tears

Rubies Climax
Written August 2007

Etheric persona
wielding sapphire's liquid fire

Volcanic magnets to feminine wiles

Uninterrupted
manifestation rivals divinity

Vow of Reclamation
Written July 22, 2005

I tolerate the game
awaiting resurrection of me
Strengthening with a vengeance
even your enlightened eyes can't see
Though a touch of your hand may save you,
arrogance will never let it be
As you sit upon your self made throne,
know when you fall...It shall be me

Passion's Reign (Villanelle)
Written May 3, 2005

Enlightened eyes steal me away from the mundane
Carrying me silently through an enchanted maze
Building promises of euphoria within passion's reign

His reasoning for me I can't quite ascertain
Logic screams for me to break from the haze
Enlightened eyes steal me away from the mundane

Embraced as lovers we dance on the astral plane
Akashic records immortalizing seductive plays
Building promises of euphoria within passion's reign

Wandering in lucid dreams that seem quite insane
I succumb to caresses that set my soul ablaze
Enlightened eyes steal me away from the mundane

Floating captive within ties of lust's golden chain
Heat seeks to fill our spirits in pleasurable ways
Building promises of euphoria within passion's reign

Seeking divine intervention to break my heart's bane
I struggle within the depths of his sapphire gaze
Enlightened eyes steal me away from the mundane
Building promises of euphoria within passion's reign

Wailing Torment (Villanelle)
Written June 6, 2004

Glimmering like the lights of a silent marquee
I float timeless within a vacant space of dreams
haunted by the wails of the crying banshee

Covering my ears against her soulful decree
watching as her essence brightly gleams
Glimmering like the lights of a silent marquee

Tears fall from eyes dark as the Baltic sea
as my soul constricts with silent screams
haunted by the wails of the crying banshee

Blood flows from my tongue like pouring Chablis
dripping from my chin in gruesome extremes
Glimmering like the lights of a silent marquee

Knowing life does not come with a guarantee
my mind seeks absolution with god-like themes
haunted by the wails of the crying banshee

Awakened to salvation answering my plea
I wallow in pools of salty sweat streams
Glimmering like the lights of a silent marquee
haunted by the wails of the crying banshee

Decadence
Written June 1, 2005

Crimson drops caress a single black rose
a mirror of blood seeping a shadow's woes
blinding pain filled eyes as they decompose
from a shallow grave of which no one knows

As the tide quickly rose from the raging sea
phantoms of love wailed almost like a banshee
claiming the night within their torturous decree
calling upon death to claim a lost soul's debris

Upon the arrival of midnight's luminous grace
gnarled hands lift the corpse from its murky place
softly tracing the lines of a once beautiful face
before spiriting it away within the Reaper's embrace

The Perfect Tear (Lapis Tear)
Written May 24, 2005

Holding the essence of the sun, within the full moon's skies
it beckoned like passion's glance, from sultry sapphire eyes
seething with power, exuding the allure of a lover's embrace
whispering enchantments within my mind, transfixing my gaze

Emotions dancing entranced, I walked slowly towards the case
where the object of my obsession, had been so gingerly placed
slender fingers reached steadily, beneath smooth crystalline glass
emerging to place a perfect tear of Lapis Lazuli, within my grasp

Staring into the mirror, as the hollow of my throat was bedecked
I fastened the chain, wondering if our energies would interconnect
upon the grace of the wind, synchronicity's acknowledgment came
as I heard a familiar voice behind me, tenderly speaking my name

Strong hands placed upon my shoulders, gently turned me around
stroking my cheek he spoke, as his steel grey eyes traveled down
"My friend, I've paid for this precious stone and now give it to you"
"Because I have never seen such beauty, as the two of you attuned"

Flight of Autumn Leaves

Written June 20, 2005

Burnished hues
beckon winds of change
taunting frost
in the aftermath of summer
awaiting winter's chill

Touching the earth
naked trees shudder
preparing for slumber
as the wheel turns the key
manifesting the dew of rebirth

Fuchsia Dream Fiesta *(An Acrostic)*

Written May 31, 2005

Frenzied passion seethes, personified
Undulating to the rhythms of forbidden dance
Captivating crowds, as glimmering bodies taunt
Hip to hip, pulsating to the heat of desire
Sangria flows freely, through moistened lips
Inhibitions giving way to the quenching of desires
As lover's meld, unashamed upon cobblestone streets

Defying interruption, the music quickens its beat
Raging in fiery tempo, as it echoes against the night
Enveloping the town within the celebration of life
As the dancers continue to soar in vibrant hues
Mingling between the sheets of the chanting crowd

Foreigners once watching in awe, pulled to their feet
Invited within the realm of cultural enchantments
Easing them into memories of olden times, displayed anew
Seduction taking hold, as they too begin to passionately sway
Tantalized by the wicked freedom of losing themselves completely
Against the bodies of strangers, embraced in a forbidden dance

Disconnected
Written June 16, 2003

Disconnected from the world
I watch my mind fly by
people stare in wonder
but they never ask why

Perhaps if they did
I wouldn't be here
but I'm looking for a glimpse
of humanity to appear

Silent Affections
Written November 1, 2006

Silent echoes cultivate nostalgia
as though it ever left mind crevices
reminding mortality, that it still lives
in breath and blood churning in vain

Such a sacred dance in a life of what ifs
taunting perfection with society's glance
with a disdain known only to watchers
too caught in business not their own

How very many moments we've wasted
embraces left undone, words unspoken
and yet in denial, there is acceptance
of love deemed unworthy, but to whom

Searching and seeking we strive for life
within a realm few care to understand
spiritually drifting, sharing energies
longing for the bliss of waiting arms

Torment is our own illusion's mistake
freedom comes to those unsuppressed
by whims of duties and peer opinions
freedom is the spiraling wake of us

Safety Net
Written October 7th, 2005

Warmth spreads
bringing a sense of home
A sense of knowing
with his hands against me
I'm never truly alone

Popcorn drifts
mingled with laughter
and his hands reach for me
beneath the handmade quilt
to tickle my left knee

I see his smile gleaming
as he whispers, "let's eat"
sapphire eyes winking at me
I relive it all, in an instant
like it wasn't just a memory

Years have passed
yes, I'm quite older
but I'd give anything
to feel his strong hands
lightly touching my shoulder

Because there, I was safe
I was wanted, I belonged
within his heart, I was treasured
as he danced with me
to my soul searching songs

Hopscotch
Written February 23, 2005

Denial is the deepest regret
Of those who cannot fathom truth

125

Self Preservation of Heart
Written July 16th, 2005

Do you feel the tears, I can not cry
and the pain that burns me deep inside
or the sorrow that threatens to consume
as I stare out the window wanting only you

Defenses grow, an icy chill I can't contain
devouring the heat you try to spread
for I shall not suffer a broken heart
but I can and will remove you from my head.

Approaching Knights (Villanelle)
Written June 7th, 2005

Silvery sheens of steel glimmer beneath fiery torch lights
Renewing hope and faith to their homeland with pride
As we watch the approach of our beloved knights

Stained in crimson they ride through long days and nights
Armor clanking against heavy swords at their side
Silvery sheens of steel glimmer beneath fiery torch lights

Behind a flag adorned with their kingdom's crest by rights
Signifying loyalty and honor they steadily ride
As we watch the approach of our beloved knights

Keeping the old stone castle locked within their sights
Warriors brave the raging waters of the river's tide
Silvery sheens of steel glimmer beneath fiery torch lights

Women hastily prepare a feast of pleasurable delights
Trumpets sounding as crowds gather both far and wide
As we watch the approach of our beloved knights

Gates open in welcome as the waiting kingdom unites
Each heart filled with a peace that has long been denied
Silvery sheens of steel glimmer beneath fiery torch lights
As we watch the approach of our beloved knights

To Light the Stars
Written May 31st, 2006

Fascinating, helium balloons, such small colorful essences
A child's toy, a lover's dream perhaps a few get well wishes

For years, I've never understood his ritual of untying the string
as he hugged one ever so gently sneaking his secret outdoors

His whispers echoing in my mind like the tear drops on his cheek
Again, I watch him climb his ladder waving good-bye as it's released

Glistening chocolate eyes stare patiently as it floats in the sky
transfixed to the moonlit rays guiding it slowly to the heavens

As it disappeared from sight as always, he smiled and sighed
but tonight, I heard so clearly his whisper, "To light the stars"

Shimmering Black Rose (Just Listen)
Written May 21, 2006

Just Listen...

Upon a journey unknown, she rides churning within waters of emotion
past the veil that hides her tears locked in mind's protective notions

Drifting past the edge of sanity, seeking the rainbows of new life
beyond a world where she feels that there's nowhere left to hide

And there she finds a spark within steadily growing like rays of dawn
empowering the soul with strength that brings her finally, safely home

We stare in awe at her, the miracle, the gift, the treasure almost lost
and as we ask what we should do, she enlightens us with her words

Just Listen...

Talisman (Acrostic)
Written August 28, 2005

Tempered steel, forged of fire
Align the energies I require
Linger close against my flesh
Invoking the angels of defense
Summon them swiftly to my side
Manifest the shields I now desire
Ancient symbol of alchemic ways
Never reveal your secret name

Hush
Written September 29, 2005

Serenity's silence beckons everlasting
in a world of chaos awaiting change

As the human race drowns in denial
stuck in the fabric of materialism's reign

A Wistful Thought
Written August 24, 2005

She walks through fragrant air, upon wings of silken mist
reliving life in pedaled hues beneath sunshine's bliss
and as she starts to dance, winds teasing ribbons in her hair
she smiles the brightest smile, as down her cheek slips a lonely tear

White Noise
Written September 19, 2005

Before your eyes, I gleam
awaiting recognition
through thinning veils
of mundane reality
and realms of other worlds

Defiantly holding my ground
as stagnant breath
reaches for me in denial
tainting the iridescence
of my glorious form

Fading into dirty walls
unholy, retributions
of the human race
insult my brilliance
denying my existence

And yet, beneath your flesh
there too, lies a spirit
waiting to be seen
through portals chained
in ignorance and fear

I see you clearly
through enlightened eyes
mourning the ruin
of a race lost to vanity
materialism and greed

Wondering
if you shall survive
the universal shifts
without praying for death
beneath insanity

Midnight Forest
Written October 2002

Come for an afternoon stroll in the midnight forest
where fantasies run free and creatures look for us
The mermaids are singing so soft and enchanting
as fairies fly through it's so very romantic

The dragon's are resting deep inside their lairs
and the elves take up dancing in the clearing over there
There's pixies and gnomes all running around
And there goes the unicorn chasing the rainbow down

Most people can't find it, this place where they roam
for the paradise is hidden in it's midnight forest home
Don't fear the darkness, be brave, come inside
for into the darkness is where your dreams hide

Tender Hues
Written August 23, 2005

Porcelain suited in tender hues
passion and elegance, divinely infused
Tiptoed grace, whispers of love
all once represented the woman I was

Tattered and torn, gingerly reaching inside
I seek resurrection of my softer side
A warrior choking on silken tears
battling the loneliness of forgotten years

Dancing in a fun house, mirrors lining my sides
I swirl in the reality I've long denied
Emerging a Goddess within tender hues
a woman complete, divinely infused

Taunting Acceptance
Written July 14th, 2005

For a friendship of pure bliss
I've chosen to reject your kiss

With fear of shattered perfection
I refuse to go in that direction

Oh why is it that you can't see
friendship is all there will ever be

A rest within our hearts embrace
of a kinship transcending time and space

Mind Erection
Written August 21, 2005

We taunt your existence weaving elysian dreams

Embodied veils of life, wielding captivating fires,
passion's tantalizing curves of sensuality

Beauty personified, uninhibited, undefined
resurrecting thoughts from shallow tides

Summoning attention, stirring depth, undisclosed
calling waves of light, annihilating shadows

Empowered our spirits speak nonconformist tongues
filling hollows of the soul with emotional awe

Eternal lotus' in bloom pulsating energies unleashed
encircling your aura, a heightened frenzy

We are your mind's erection,
manifesting enchanted throes of ecstasy

Shoreline Beacon
Written September 5, 2004

Vigilant protector of a shoreline unseen
in the dead of night, it's your beacon I see
Above white squalls your zenith shines
a xanthic glow that always eases my mind
As it guides me keen through rocky debris
from my quest upon these jeopardous seas

Fire's Grace
Written July 31, 2003

Gliding far and wide, belonging to no land
is a wonder to behold, the flaming bird of Aér'aí'chán

Through centuries it lives barely bothering to rest
more graceful than a swan, it's beauty golden red

The essence of the sun makes up it's fiery wings
slender of beak, full of tail, a sweet mournful song it sings

To stare into its eyes, you're a lucky soul indeed
to be allowed to view it's inner mysteries

With the stroke of your hand upon it's splendid glory
you shall be healed and left with no worries

But should an injustice you do upon mankind
the phoenix will shriek upon you a mighty cry

Drowning your screams as it's fire consumes
talons pierce your skin, justice served your doom

Once every five hundred years it's mystical song breaks your heart
as the bird's internal fires blaze and its soul prepares to depart

Burning within it's own cleansing fire until it is completely consumed
to rise from the ashes in three days reborn, ready to take flight anew

Daring a Dream
Written September 5, 2005

I feel your touch and quiver, longing for sweet release
Though it comes in droves, next to my body, there's no heat
No arms to curl within, no chest on which to lay my head
No lips to touch the softness of mine, no hands caressing my hair

So I ask you this, phantom lover in the night
Why should I give you my body let alone my heart and soul
for when daylight comes it brings the emptiness
that keeps me from being whole

Last Tear
Written February 16, 2004

As my last tear drop falls, I say upon the raging winds
the words of my soul of which you never listened.
Unburdening my heart and releasing the pain
from the hold that binds me from living life once again.

You used and abused a trust that was pure,
tortured a heart that has long been yours,
filled a life with dreams waiting on reality
for what you knew would never be

Look in the mirror into your green eyes
and tell me the truth can you face all your lies
will guilt consume you for the heart that you crushed
to run off in a hurry following only your lust

Will you regret the love that you cast aside
when the other leaves you lonely wishing you would die
Karma will come to you swift and sure to your side
carrying with it all my love and every tear that I've cried

And I shall be golden, a great tower of strength
flying beyond the indigo and healing my wings
As you wallow once more in the abyss that you'll lay
upon the day that you crushed all the promises once made.

Tink's Dance in Neverland
Written April 30, 2005

Beyond the chapters that were written, there is life beyond myth
In a land of timeless wonders, where fantasy shall always live
Grand parties gracing mountains by the singing mermaid's stream
where rainbows shine upon earth, clouds of darkness, rarely seen

Captain Hook's been defeated, the pirates lost in ocean's waves
and Peter Pan mourns the memory of Wendy Lady, flown away
The Indian Princess, to cheer him, planned a ball of feast and games
and as the moon shines down, upon a splendid vision they all gazed

Against the tallest tree, Tink floats quite vibrant, shimmering starlight
staring Peter down with love as he stares in awe that she's alive
Her gown, elegant emerald green wings poised in splendor to seduce
barefoot, she starts to dance to the wind's enchanting tune

Peter moves to her side, entranced never has her beauty been more pure
as he reaches out his hand to her his heart falls victim to her allure
And there in his palm she beams, wings bursting colors of autumn leaves
as Peter leans to kiss her softly realizing she's the woman of his dreams

The Fairy Queen, gleefully watches hidden behind the sacred oak
and upon the midnight hour she grants the wish that Tink had hoped
Swirls of mist, carrying her tiny frame, laying her softly upon the earth
as she transforms into a human granting love's bliss, upon rebirth

The fantasy of Neverland spins on with Tink dancing again, in Peter's arms
chapters of adventures to unfold, a mother for the lost boys' finally come
Upon the clearest nights an amber light flickers, beckoning us all
to reach beyond the mundane, to Neverland with our happy thoughts

Spiritual Stirrings of My Inner Child
Written May 31st, 1999

Through a child's eyes I remember
always knowing there was more...
far more than the hypocrites that sang
of Jesus and his undying love

I watched them all as they cast me out,
my eyes too bright, my stare too sturdy
a child with age old essence
waiting for something to fill me fully

There was no church to hold me
no congregation to ease my soul
but when I stepped into the wind
my spirit began to soar

Upon the waters I stared
as they whispered to me
the fire of the sun caressed
against the earth, I felt its energy

Laying at night in silence
I gazed upon the shimmering stars
as spirits came in droves to speak
of mysteries that I've always known

The God source speaks to me
as I raise my arms for its embrace
Through the forces of nature
that come coursing through my veins

I need no church, nor its rules
or books interpreted by man
within the solace of my mind
I find the answers to all my questions

Spirituality is in everything I feel and see
the rocks, the grass, the singing birds
a child's laughter, an old man's tears
hearts unbound with religion's curse

At peace I live within the essence
of what spirituality should always bring
peace of mind, serenity of heart
with the love and respect of everything

Entranced by the Dragon
Written May 8, 2004

Spell bound they blindly stare
never really knowing why
drawn into mysterious beams
shining from enlightened eyes

Feeling the essence of power
they can't accept or understand
as they wander what it is
trapped inside this woman

They don't know your voice
feel your wings embrace
can not fathom your desire
or the wisdom of your race

Ancient powers stir inside
waves of healing in my being
flowing out my hands in light
internal fire, they aren't seeing

The dragon deep within
is what they'll never see
though they come in droves
whenever they're in need

And once their need is gone
illness forgotten and faded away
they leave me to myself
to face another lonely day

But I don't mind getting lost
carried upon the dragon's wings
through the astral spirals
as I listen to Akasha sing

So carry me away once more
blue eyed guardian of my soul
mysteries await us in the ethers
it's time to put humanity on hold

Beyond the Blackened Mirror
Written July 21, 2005

Haphazard waste
never taunted me the way you do
looking through half closed eyes
insistently defiant

Ranges of your moods
swinging like chandeliers
made of glass and brass
tormenting each other, as they shatter
like time's hour glass

Nostalgia's mirror
long cracked in the heat
leaving me sated
in a flame of unquenched curiosity
gilded and framed

While phantoms of you
lingering on insanity's edge
merely toy, like a lost illusion
leaking the black tar of fears upon me
as you stain my pane

I often wonder
in which realm of reality
you stalk peasant's dreams
weaving webs of fantasy
from freshly torn veins

And then I gaze
past the puffiness of your eyes
into the awaiting iris
that reveals lost secrets
of your soul

Realizing what's hidden
behind sheens of sarcasm
storing callous misrepresentations
is the illumination of self
you've never revealed

Sacrilegious Love
Written June 18, 2005

You sculpted me to suit you,
to be all and everything
you've ever wanted me to be

Forged by your hands
filled with your heart's love
your goddess for eternity

You brought me to life
with tender desperation
yearning for great love

I can never be taken away
for I am the one woman
you've always dreamed of

I possess all that you willed
for you made me as I am
but your soul, you have forsaken

You defied the laws of nature
your heart shall once again grieve
for my love was not given, but taken

My touch on your flesh is cold
I've no blood within my veins
no heat to keep you warm

I am merely water and clay
the unholy abomination
of which your priest warned

Yet, I stand before you still
remember, I am your creation
the woman of your dreams

Will you cast me back to stone
or take me in your arms
and make love to the beast

A Vampire's Revelation
Written June 14, 2005

You sought to covet the great divine of my shadows
yet the fear of my light was forsaken by your arrogance
though nocturnal, does God's light not shine upon me
I am but a beast amongst the food chain, the same as you
as cattle is to your stomach, so your blood shall be to mine
I am the closest to god that shall ever be
for on the very essence of his creations I dine

Like an angel I walk, watching the world change
humanity disappearing behind soulless eyes
my beauty bewitching, until you want to be me
stalking me on the chance that I may take your life
shudder in my embrace and gaze into my eyes
stare into the history of the human race and tell me
do you really want to live for all time

Shudder of Love's Death
Written July 6, 2004

In the requiem's solace I took no blame
for promises once made within lovers haste
but laid gently upon the thorns bestowed
of a heart transformed to a blackened rose
And there, with the thinning streams of blood
that threatened to taint and jade my soul
I conjured the sweetest wine ever tasted
with the saline of my eyes' etheric glow

How it caressed my tongue, I have no words
for euphoria it killed within a sanctity so pure
that the little death of lust's fleeting release
was but a chime upon the wind to be heard
Returning the innocence of a new born babe
immortal to the realms of androgynous rebirth
upon an ageless mind, carrying ancient ways
reviving my spirit to again walk the earth

139

Defiance
Written 1998

You may bruise my body
and torture my mind
but my soul lives forever
and my body will die

Defying the Devil's Grasp
Written June 17, 2004

Shards of glass pinion me
against clouds of darkest gray
daring me to rise again
from depressions wary gaze

Cutting through tendons and veins
as though they were death's tease
absorbing the numbness of my pain
leaving it gripping my broken body

I pray upon the light to save me
as the hands of fate steadily squeeze
but my wounded cries fall upon deaf ears
it seems the angels have forsaken me

The devil waits with bated breath
to hear my cry for sweet release
and though he drools to own my soul
I'll never give in to the beast

What once I loved and so adored
he's taken with a smiling face
so suffer I do and fight I shall
knowing within my final moments
I shall reclaim my grace

Enchanted Land of Wanderlust
Written June 10, 2004

Seeking serenity I walked through a valley of dreams
beyond the enchanted cliffs to where the Mermaids sing
Gazing at the shimmering of their emerald tails and eyes
as they sang of all the creatures they've encountered in their time

The sun shone brightly down but a shadow came my way
looking up I spied a dragon within its claws, a light blue egg
A majestic, golden splendor carried upon black tipped wings
heading for the highest cave to make a home for its new babe

Just then, a bright green apple appeared like magic in my hand
and as I stared in wonder laughter drifted through the air
I looked to see a wizard dark of hair, in purple robes
walking steadily towards me with a tiny little gnome

They greeted me with smiles and a friendly shake of the hand
telling me to offer the apple to the sun and streaming wind

And to my outstretched hand came the most beautiful sight
two unicorns, mother and child with coats of the purest white
They stunned my joyous eyes with an essence so divine
as they nibbled from the apple gently eating, one at a time

I then sat upon the lush green grass as they let me touch their grace
and blessed me with good luck with a brush of their silken manes
My new friends came to join me in pure bliss, we laughed and played
as the dragon chased a rainbow by the stream as the mermaids sang

Then once the sun sank down to kiss waters of green and blue
I laid my head upon the grass whispering hello to the moon
And as I drifted off to sleep faeries sprinkled me with their dust
to protect me as I roamed in dreams within their land of wanderlust

Ghost Child
Written June 1993

Last night I dreamt of you again
only to wake up all alone
I could feel you near me
drifting through our home

There was no one to hold me
as I cried my lonely tears
but the memory of you came
and with it brought my fears

I wonder sometimes what I'm missing
never holding you in my arms
I never meant to lose you
but I couldn't keep you from harm

Perhaps I should have fought harder
and cared for myself more
I never thought that he would hit me
little did I know what was in store

I remember thinking you were there
and wondering how it would be
I loved you before I knew you
but it was never meant, I see

I never got to hold you once
but in my dreams you are around
sometimes I hear your cries
other times there is no sound

Inside I'm silently longing
that perhaps a child I will bear
of course it can never replace you
you were my first, my little prayer

I don't know if I can be a mom
people tell me that I could
but I don't feel much like a woman
even though I know I should

I wake up alone every single day
hiding my fears, trying to make a life
but the truth is my ghost child
I don't think I'll ever be a wife

Spirit Without A Cloud

Written November 8, 2003

Moon drop candy kisses
and double edge swords
call seductively from the shadows
of where my heart was torn

Violins never played
the dirge of drowning souls
as I wept tears of blood
upon the gown I wore

Holding in my hands
the pulse of my life force
I stare into the blackened eyes
of a face with no remorse

Sweet victim of the truth
passed upon a fading wind
come to collect the toll
for a journey with no end

Light beckons behind a veil
though darkness blocks my way
my strength begins to fail
as my mind starts to stray

A mournful song I hear
sending chills along my spine
the shadow comes to claim me
but yet my will is mine

Oh Wraith within my path
I command thee to leave
for I have known your song
for many centuries

I laugh in your face of fury
and spit upon your brow
without my fear you're nothing
but a spirit without a cloud

Race the Flame
Written November 2, 2003

Gasoline pools flicker
beneath the moon light
as black candles burn
threatening to ignite

Dripping their essence
to float among the sea
of the fuel to the fire
that is yet to be

A timer of fate
glimmering in the wind
a beckon for those
who created the sin

Come forward and swim
in the stench and get high
play Russian roulette
with the beast of the night

Looking for absolution
of a self wrought hell
changing your mind
at the toll of church bells

Racing the flame
lit to set you free
reaching to snuff it
liquid dripping, you scream

Drifting in agony
swimming in pain
a burning pile of flesh
with no one to blame

Ashes to ashes
dust turned to mud
a prelude to nothing
another song left unsung

Voodoo
Written October 2, 2003

Who do the Voodoo? My mans run amuck.
I ain't gotta live chicken but I got a darnn duck.
I reckon I ought not go shouting this way,
but I'm over his crap now that man's gonna pay

You do the Voodoo? Can ya whammy my man?
I been up all night waitin' on him again.
I ain't got no money, rotten snake took it all.
But I'll give ya my jewelry just to watch him crawl,

Won't ya please do the Voodoo? Here's a piece of his hair,
a bloody old band-aid and his favorite underwear.
I ain't worried for karma it's done took too long.
The rat bastards been cheatin since the day he was born.

You'll do the Voodoo? Oh, yes ma'am, take it all.
I don't need the weddin ring, it don't mean nothin at all/
All the love I had inside left years ago.
I been plannin and waitin til the kids was grown

So you do the Voodoo, I'll go pack his bags.
Cause he's meetin the door when he comes back.
He says I'm dumber than jello, reckon he might be right.
But I'll be laughin and dancing as he loses his mind.

Long live the Voodoo, cause it's saving my life.
He don't want a divorce so I'll be a dead man's wife.

Thanks for the voodoo.

My Native Love
Written June 11, 2005

Dying embers of the sun
caress smooth bronze skin
lingering against the power
of his taunt muscled frame

I admire his beauty

Heart beats quicken
anticipation rising in the night
as he steadily approaches
eyes, seething with desire

His strength fuels my soul

Amber boring into green
needing no words to follow
as strong hands encircle me
full lips claiming mine

Freeing the sorrow that claims me

Falling upon cool sands
entwined in passion's heat
we meld to the rhythm of lust
spirits soaring beyond time

Seeing beyond flesh and bones

Sheens of sweat glimmer
burnt sienna, by firelight
as soft whispers of love
breath against my silken neck

To claim the loving spirit below

Against each other we lay
serenely drifting on sleep's waves
awaiting the rising of the sun
to grace our love's embrace

Desperation
Written January, 2002

Once the bed is empty the heart seeks
that in which it failed to keep
though poison its touch may have been
we crave it for a lifetime of sin
What lingers is wanton lust, hope and pain
pushing us along through life's little game
just to see what's left for it to destroy
when love is questioned and you feel like a toy

Hypocrite
Written January 1998

Victim of the past, crying over naught
Violation of your soul is something self wrought
What you seek as absolution you hold within
Yet you drown everyday for what you consider sin.

A Lover's Lie
Written June 9, 2004

As the stars melt into the sun
I gaze upon the colors of the sea
remembering what it once felt like
when your arms wrapped around me
and you softly whispered
"I'll always want only you"

Stalking Prey
Written April 26, 2005

Is it her fear you sense?

Staring wide eyed, concealed
as though poising for flight
mind seemingly in a daze
cowering before you in the night

Or has arrogance deceived you?

Her passive stance, a clever guise
clouding your mind, as she stares
conjuring enchantments, hidden
palms open, partaking energies there

Are you truly the hunter?

Standing, smiling in shadow clouds
moving towards what calls desire
claiming her within your arms
only to perish in the depth of her fire

Or have you fallen prey?

Walking steadily from your side
ashes streaking through the wind
seductive laughter rules your mind
the game finally over, she wins

Tell me, do you feel all powerful now?

My Cherubs (Jacob & Jessie)
Written June 17, 2005

Tiny faces giggle in unison.
How could I resist?
Reaching to hold two angels,
waiting to hug and kiss.

Refreshingly Charmed
June 17, 2005

I struggled,
against devilish delight
refusing to succumb
to silver haunting bells
stroking against porcelain walls
as they taunted me

Laughter echoed,
from smiling, milky faces
reaching towards me
as they beckoned
with clumsy, tiny hands
poised at my lips

Madness came,
swiftly claiming me
with cool sea green sensations
penetrating willing lips
as it mingled with chocolate
melting against my tongue

In release,
I grinned in satisfaction,
giggling against a spoon of love
as it playfully slid from my lips
into the mouth of babes
carrying mint charms
saying, I love you

Sweets and Salt
Written June 8, 2005

Cravings for sweets overtook me
wandering along sandy sea shores
ocean spray rising to cling to me
as I licked my lips, tasting salt

My silent mind began to wander
old memories coming in floods
of holding my brother's hand
eating ice cream, rocky road

How we loved to visit vendors
displayed on boardwalk's peaks
selling cinnamon roasted almonds
and tons of other tasty treats

Stopping to nestle in the sands
enjoying private moments locked away
visions of pastel coated almonds
gave way to images of his wedding day

How handsome he was, as he danced
holding his bride within his arms
smiling at each other within a dream
like satin swirls of black and almond

Feeling at peace within nostalgia
I rose, beginning the long walk home
lighter of heart and full of life
thankful to cravings of sweets and salt

Steel Blue Tremors
Written June 3, 2004

Boring through my soul
heating me like a flame
riveted to the spot I stood
as you whispered softly
nothing but my name

Such a beautiful caress
to the depths of my ear
and a thrill to an old heart
long thought to be dead
bringing me silently to tears

Steel blue that won't lie
waiting patiently for my smile
I beg you not to touch me
else my morals may leave
with passion long denied

Though fingers want to caress
as soft lips gently roam
to love you would be sweet death
but the key to your heart
I fear, I shall never own

Soul mates we are truly
but our time shall never be
fates made our decision for us
within the temporal solace
of our silent memory

Vow of Silence
Written August 27, 2005

Poetic, lies the secrets
of pristine ladies
locked in regal moments
of a iridescent mirage

The sanctuary of friendship
untouched by reality
as fate deals its hand
within the brilliance of loyalty

Cadence ripples the shroud
of dignity pictured in blushed hues
concealing clandestine meetings
upon the garden terrace

Virgin robes left enraptured
waiting for destiny to beckon
with gentle wings
brushing misgivings away

As dreams of a proper marriage
waif upon whims of fancy
conjuring an embrace of hope
with child-like wonder

Society forgotten
momentarily they pause
reflecting joyous moments
nearly lost in tainted speculation
silenced only by the breath of time

Regrets
Written January 2003

I have fought within myself, the demons within
traveled throughout time to the lives I've been in

I've stirred in chaos and rode the waves
of emotional banter and evil ways

Looked deep into souls including mine
counting the misery I'd left behind

It's so easy to hurt yet hard to be nice
when you're so cold your heart turns to ice

Then the day comes. the shield does break
you're bitter and lonely from cruel mistakes

You look through the window again at your soul
and find the hearts gone all that's left is a hole

Your living and breathing yet feel like a corpse
again void of emotions, your life way off course

Suddenly a savior beckons and calls
but you're too frozen to care at all

All that you have is a life of "what ifs"
if only you'd given in to love's first kiss

Let Me Touch You
Written January 4, 2003

Let me touch you with my eyes
searching deep into your soul
falling into the swirling mist
sharing the secrets we know

Let me touch you with my hands
wiping from you all your tears
moving softly against your skin
caressing away your deepest fears

Let me touch you with my mouth
kissing away the pain you feel
taking you into a fantasy
enveloping you in a love so real

Let me touch you with my mind
for I know you can understand
sharing myself completely with you
showing you who I was and who I am

Let me touch with my heart
for this I offer freely to you
let us grow forever with each other
making each day of life fresh and new

Let me touch you with all my senses
sharing my life force with you
as we wrap around each other
our beauty completely fills the room

Sacred Ground
January 7, 2003

Inside you're stirring
the energy flows
you hear the moon calling
tonight we all go

A top of the mountain
where the local folk shun
to gather together
with the moon to be one

The clearing is set
and the bonfire lit
there's laughter and singing
soon the dancing begins

As we all gather round
in a circle we move
to chant with each other
and draw down the moon

The colors they fly
as the energies stir
the quarters are present
and the priestess is heard

The circle does glow
as our energies meld
Our focus together
as we cast the spell

The goddess is with us
and she's smiling down
to bless her children
on this sacred ground

Once Again Risen
Written January 15, 2003

I have risen like the phoenix
from the ashes of your fires
destined by fate to live
with unfulfilled desires

I soar above the chaos
you sought to leave behind
driven by the fury
of your stream of endless lies

Filtering through debris
from the explosion of my heart
laughing as I roam free
from the life you tore apart

In me is the strength
you shall never find
it cannot be destroyed
by your simple little mind

All you could take is gone
dead, lost or faded away
you have no power over me
no matter what you do or say

I've awakened from the shadows
I claim myself once more
suffer your own fate my friend
for I am no longer yours

My power is timeless
and it comes without sin
I've found what I lost with you
the goddess that dwells within

Fear
Written January 18, 2005

I hover in the shadows
you know me oh, too well
I am the one that keeps you
locked into your private hell

I feed upon your weakness
and strengthen all your flaws
I'm the one you can not see
yet you're wrapped within my claws

I whisper in your ear
as you try to take flight
dear, sweet darling child
stay with me again tonight

Together we've built a wall
that the others can not see
our fortress is secure
as long as you stay with me

I'll keep you from the world
all tight and locked away
you don't want to go there
listen to me dear, obey

Stay far from the pretty lights
the smiles and the games
they'll only break your heart again
you'll have no one left to blame

I'll bind your heart again
to keep it from the pain
and when you die a lonely death
they'll say it was all in vain

But you and I shall know
the truth from all their lies
they just couldn't see you
clutched by the fear inside

Crimson Farewell
Written July 20, 2003

Sitting upon a shattered wall
surrounded by thorns
acid rain stinging my face
quenching misery's thirst

Neon tears flow from my eyes
looking much like radiator fluid
as my hands do animation
of what I think of this world

My mind is a vat of junk on fire
spraying ashes amongst mankind
of feelings that I purposely burnt
to leave you all behind

I make my stand upon the wall
to the sky I raise my bleeding arms
slipping in my own sweet blood
I die, falling upon the bed of thorns

Echoes of the Mundane
Written August 20, 2005

Star lights trail chaos
beneath life's snow
imprisoned
conjuring dim realities
of society's bliss

Billowing winds
of denial's chants
answer in overcasts
forcing change
of sublime dementia

Hollow laughter remains

Lonely Vamp
Written August 3, 2003

Come join me in my coffin
there's room enough for two
all you need is a little faith
and you'll be immortal too

Don't fear my lusty bite
for sweet pleasure you'll obtain
if only you care to venture near
and politely offer me a vein

I'm so bored with all the hunting
the chasing down of evil men
I want to settle down at night
and play the hostess once again

I live in such a lovely home
a sacred guardian at my gates
I long for a much more festive life
won't you please come be my mate

Together we shall rule the night
and play all sorts of games
of course we shall still have to feed
but hey, that's our claim to fame

Wolf's Bane (Acrostic)
Written September 6, 2003

Witches use me for protection
Of the creatures of the night
Lizard skin wrapped around me
Forms invisibility, carried tight
Brew me for a werewolf
Swiftly calling upon Hecate
Aconite swiftly cures their disease
Never eat me though, my mortal friend
Excruciating death, you will incur

I am Enigma
Written September 7, 2003

I am the devil, candy coated, staring you in the face
waiting to rip out your heart, isn't that what you think

The evil witch with no soul, eyes shining like steel
born with no conscience, devoid of God's will

Go ahead and beat me, purge me of the evil I make
kill the baby inside me saving it from my fate

You've never seen inside me, I'm what you want me to be
trying to survive in a world of glass houses and memories

My heart bleeds everyday, I crave to be in someone's arms
to wake up just one time knowing I'm safe and loved

I dream of kittens and children laughing and playing outside
wanting to be called Mommy and fill this void I have inside

I am ice cream in chains, a wonder behind an iron wall
wanting to be melted away and taken from misery's call

I am a natural healer, aware, full of beauty and loving light
hidden beneath life's trials wanting to rest instead of fight

My body aches for release, to soar wild and free in the sky
longing to spread my colors like a phoenix in the night

I sing a beautiful song all the time that no one ever seems to hear
I grow more weary everyday, all I want right now is to just disappear

Denied Stone
Written September 14, 1998

I'm choking on the words
I just can't seem to say
though my heart speaks
I keep those words at bay

They've always betrayed me
when spoken without doubt
used against me like swords
as they rip my soul out

Then I'm locked in a world
very few understand
clawing my way back
until I once again stand

On the threshold of sanity
tattered, with red glaring eyes
the shadow of who I once was
locked hidden inside

Waiting and lurking
for a chance to tame the beast
with the faint glimmer of hope
in the very core of my being

Losing years of my life
for a dream we all chase
of a world filled with love
lost to my tongue's haste

So I'll sit here and stare
silently as my heart bleeds
knowing I'll never tell you
just how much you mean to me

Depth Impaired
Written August 23, 2003

Does it haunt you in your fitful sleep
cellophane lace , a feast for your eyes
sugar walls melting within a rainbows grasp

Seeking retribution for the vapors woven
in a sky of endless illusions
of what was but yet has never become

Beaten by society, the wicked tongue of deceit
embedded in shards, exploded from the ice
holding the sanity of the mind

Leaving breathless the contempt
searching for perfection to release the conscience
from purgatory of self inflicted fears

Does it make sense? Of course not
You never see beyond the words you read
letting them explore your senses and shallow mind

Flushed
Written September 1, 1998

A candy wrapper floating in the wind
Landing, run over stuck to your shoe again

Only the outer shell, all the good stuff gone
Destination unknown, merely tagging along

Trod through the streets from pleasure to pain
Bliss to misery, Isn't it all the same

Scraped off on the curb, left tattered and torn
A memory lost in life's raging storm

Shadowed – Gift or Curse?
Written August 30, 2003

They come when I least expect
flowing into my mind
whether awake or sleeping
information that can't be denied

Spiraling into submission
worming their way to my mouth
flowing from my lips
without hesitation or doubt

Truths masked by egos
that people just can't see
a mirror of themselves unchecked
being played for all to see

They beg to the know the truth
a glimpse into the unforeseen
though I deliver what they want
they delve not into the mystery

Depth escapes the conscious thought
emotions block the truth
do they really want to know the future
or do they seek only to be amused

They seek me only to haunt me
behind my back, labeling me a freak
but they never fail to come to me
when a healer or advice they seek

To lock my door imprisoned
a lonely person I would be
but to live with a gift not treasured
sometimes brings the greatest misery

Missing Nothing
Written September 14, 2003

Artistic visions slaughtered with careless words
of those that never saw what needed to be heard
drones of voices haunting day and night
from those that see the world as only black and white

Technicolor dreams long faded away
leaving behind mists of shadows and decay
warping a mind that people didn't understand
making a zombie out of what once was a man

Now indifference passes on a borrowed chance
to walk back into the world or forever be damned
and though the soul seeks only to be free
the body falters blindly willing itself unseen

Sinking and withering into insanity's edge
no hunger, no thirst, all passions are dead
if the heart knew the soul was about to take flight
a tear might have fallen from darkened eyes

The crow cries but once in the morning light
carrying the call of another ended life
though the stench fills the streets carried on the winds
no one takes notice and a new day begins

Etheric Warrior
Written September 23, 2003

I beckon you with gilded wings, singing enchantments on the wind
A ray of hope to lead you back from the abyss you've dwelled within

Though you fear me more than battle, I shall quench your heart's desire
heal your wounds and free your bonds, casting your demons to the fire

Stare through me, my dark angel, bore deep into my soul
feel my light envelope you, let my love for you take hold

We are the perfect balance, the blessed darkness and the light
A splendid cloud of blissful gray between the worlds of black and white

164

Cutting the Tether
Written September 15, 2003

Are you wallowing again?

Stuck in the abyss you made yourself
upon the edge of a glass wall
bleeding from the eyes that refuse to see
you, yourself have caused your fall

Trying to suck the life from me
as you drown in self inflicted pain
refusing to see the light before you
believing the gods have forsaken you again

Reality no longer serves you
perception lost inside your narrow mind
once broad with intelligence and hope
turned from gold to dust in a few months time

What is it that you seek from me
company within the misery of your cell
once our life together was a rainbow
but you went and shot it all to hell

Poor pitiful you, I'm no longer crying
as you cling to your own chains
when the world became too real
and took all your excuses away

Go ahead and wallow there my love
I've no energy left for you
You want me near, release the fears
there's really nothing left for me to do

I love you...but I don't need you

Save yourself!

Autumn's Enchantment
Written September 16, 2003

The wheel turns and all things change
reflecting the cycle of life
thunderstorms and hurricanes
sunny days turn to chilly air
the sour becomes sweet
and returns to the earth
waiting to again reclaim it's place
upon the showers of spring
and green pastures ahead

What is lost is found hibernating
waiting for the ice to thaw
and though the brisk winds call
the bliss of sleep makes its claim
as healing spreads throughout
fueling the dawn of a new age
a new time for us to reckon with
and explore it's brilliance
through eyes wide open

At the dawn of rebirth

Realization of Loneliness
Written 2002

A recluse waiting on borrowed time
searching for a little piece of mind
leans his hand upon the window sill
hoping a solemn breeze to feel
he wishes the sun to hit his face
and yet his foot won't leave its space
As the damned memories come to play
like a broken record all night and day

Jealousy's Prize
Written September 22, 2003

I see it all from the pedestal you've placed me on in vain
Moonbeams struck your heart and I'll never be the same

You've taken me to places I never wanted to see
To shut me down in sorrow, taking away my heart's key

Wearing me like a frame, a pretty picture of your own
Spinning tales of wonders that have yet to unfold

My spirit roamed so freely until the green eyed monster came
Placing me in this fortress alone to watch the world fade away

All the love I held has withered into seething fires of hate
Ah yes, rest well my love, for tonight I shall escape

Please
Written September 29, 2003

Burn my heart to cinders, cast my soul into the sea
Bury my body where you will, these things I no longer need

My mind has long since left, replaced by a pit of air
I'm only wandering aimlessly along the path to nowhere

Feet not touching the ground never knowing why
Clinging to the gnawing ache I feel so deep inside

I plead to you release me from these earthy ties
I'd do it myself but I'm too weak, believe me, I have tried

Cast my ashes to the winds, set my wounded soul free
Do it swift, do it sure, but do it now, have mercy

167

Ruined
Written October 5, 2003

Whispers and echoes, seas against shores
grave billowing winds, a disenchanted whore

Wavering silver strings, threads holding to life
teasingly beckoning through mental strife

Revelations, realizations, retributions of time
burning sorrow, blinding pain, all intrusive but mine

Burning bridges to nowhere, a sweet little bane
past screams of torture comforting the insane

Tears of blood, heart of gold, steely snake eyes
glaring with depth, pleading, daring demise

A vacancy once filled, scents of misplaced desire
eradicated in a moment, no longer required

I Do
Written May 4, 2004

Quench my thirst
with the honey of your lips
poisoning me to submission
within your eyes
give me one glimpse
into the prism of your soul
the essence of your hues
and as my heart explodes
won't you whisper to me
"I do"

168

Jumbled
Written September 30, 2003

If I only had the words to tell you, I'd scream deep within your mind
For your ears no longer hear any words of mine

You can't know me because you never took the time
to sit back and delve into the recesses of my mind

If I could only make you see the things you never could
I'd show you all the things in me that you've never understood

You can't own me, I'm not for you to take
There's nothing that chains me to the life you choose to make

If only I could make you stop seeing only the bad in life
I'd wrap you up within my arms and be your blessed wife

You can't guilt me, I've nothing to be guilty for
I tried to save us a million times but I can't take anymore

If only you would read this and know how hard I fight
to keep myself from leaving you through the days and nights

You can't feel me drowning in the tears I hold inside
but will you finally reach for me once my heart has died

If only I could save you from the torment of your soul
I know our love would once again fill your heart and make us whole

The Banishing
Written March 2004

Empowered tools of the rite
beckon in an enchanted dance
of illumination upon us all
energies called to heal release
as golden flames turn to onyx
banishment granted by the gods

Riding the Spirals Home
Written October 6, 2003

You beckon to me so I can no longer deny
things inside of me that I tried so hard to hide
The pull of your essence, the tug of your embrace
bind me to the mysteries of another time and place

Earth heal my wounds, Air expand my weary mind
Fire bring me courage, Water balance me inside
I walk between the worlds healing my broken wings
back where I belong, where my soul always sings

Quicken my faded spirit with the powers that be
let them meld again with the ones inside of me
Earth keep me steady, Air provide insight
Fire fuel my passions, Water cleanse me this night

Free the tainted locks cast upon my crimson doors
let the indigo shine free, make me whole once more
Akasha shine upon my face leading my way home
where upon your spiraling tides I shall forever roam

Hug of Truth
Written November 3, 2003

How dare you entrance me and ruin my perfect world
Sliding into my heart when I finally felt good
Taking away the illusion that I was doing okay
And leaving me lacking in what to do or say

How dare you look at me with eyes of azure blue
that bore into my soul awakening something new
Bringing forbidden dreams to haunt me day and night
Just when I thought my life was beginning to turn out right

How dare you hold me within your arms of steel
making me feel secure for the first time in years
What should I tell him, are you really for real
Or are you here to show me just how I truly feel

How dare you make me doubt what I've waited so long for
My heart melts when you smile as my soul begins to soar
I thought I was so happy and I'd never find a greater love
but in an instant it was shattered in the embrace of a friendly hug

Slamming the Door
Written 2000

Your love may quicken my heart and soul
but it is only I that can make myself whole

Stand away from me now, I am not ashamed
to follow my soul and throw you away

171

The Pentacle of Me
Written April 12, 2004

I hear it singing to me, the power of the elements
daring me to dance to their never ending tune

I feel them surge inside of me with each breath I take
and know that now, after all this time, we are once again in tune

I am the power of the Earth, the healing flows through my hands
building and guiding me to use it's special gift

I am the power of Air riding the indigo spirals
collecting ancient knowledge to see and hear what's required

I am the power of Fire a tower of courage and strength
with a passion for life to survive anything that comes my way

I am the power of Water , waves of intuition awakening
cleansing away emotional debris as past lives stir inside of me

I am Akasha, the Spirit, for it flows within my soul
spreading everlasting light, balancing me, making me whole

For I am the Pentacle from which I draw my strength
blessed and empowered, a star child full of beauty and grace

Free Will
Written July 11, 2005

There's a light in my soul you can never take away
A spirit deep inside me that you will never break
There's a love in my heart that you shall never kill
You have no power over me.
I control my own free will.

172

I Shouldn't Have Dared...But I Did
Written May 5, 2004

The tinkling of wind chimes lulled me
though the dragon within warned me
and the wolf tried to keep me at bay
I closed my eyes and ventured
into a new strange and sacred place

I knew you were there, yes I saw you
though you tried to hide behind the veil
your gasp of breath carried on a breeze
as you eased in the shadows
it was destined to reach my delicate ears

I wanted to touch your hand
and gaze deep into your dark eyes
but stood riveted in silence
a tiny smile gracing my face
as I tried to reach you with my mind

For there I could touch your face
feel the softness of your cheek
run my fingertip across your lips
as my aura mingled with yours
and we shared our energies

You felt me then, I felt you shudder
as though a chill had touched your soul
I knew not to approach you physically
my intentions intrigued, yet you feared
the essence of my brazen reality

I know I shouldn't have dared to come, but I did
so upon the wind I leave an invitation, only for you
hear it with serenity, the choice is yours
the universe knows, I speak to you truth

Meld with me willingly, sweet beauty
your fierceness I do not fear nor taunt
my desires androgynous, not lust
I'm only drawn to you, I want to know you
no tricks, no lies only perfect love and trust

Mirrored Animosity
Written May 7, 2004

Oh, I wouldn't want to be you, to be waiting
on the verge of a mind about to collapse
a soul preparing to delve into an abyss
that you, yourself devised to manifest

Did you think I would cower before you
depleted of power and devastated of heart
begging forgiveness of what I did not create
and wallowing in pools of my own blood

As you sat suffering from sweet delusions
of me crawling naked before your tin throne
throwing myself upon the blade of your mercy
as I screamed for release from my pain

I stood in power, laughing at your attempt
standing before your demons, commanding
calling them by name and sending them back
upon you with their fury, as my strength grew

Be warned of who you play with and what you send
for the sheer amusement of your broken soul
know the power you abuse shall turn on you
leaving you rotting in self wrought defeat

There are those, like me, that know, that feel
those that sense the second you utter your phrases
they are ancient and timeless, more powerful than you
who dwell in peace, yet do not falter to defend

The universe will not condone your actions, nor whims
and I shall reign untouchable, at peace and without fear
as the ancient guardians commence to shatter you
for all you've done unjustly, in vain to destroy me

And I shall watch in silence with one lone tear
slowly dripping down the cheek of my silken face
no remorse or regret, just a small bit of sadness
for your humanity lost and the power you used in vain

The Rise and Fall of Happiness
Written May 2004

She prayed for someone to hold and take the loneliness away
staring out the window as the rains began to sing

Upon her came the light, everlasting in it's glory
telling her to trust the one that she had met this morning

And as the light shone down, quickening her faith
she stared into the ethers for the future that was paved

But had she known the ending, would she have opened her heart
Yes, love came true in splendor and then tore her life apart

Artic Lust
Written April 2004

Come closer into my realm but not yet within my space
flaunting your perfection within the smile of my grace

Amused with the melody of laughter coming from your poisoned lips
I seek to watch your body move through the turmoil of our sins

I've tamed the beast inside of me from the passion of my heart
quickened with painful betrayal threatening to tear my world apart

And from it I've begun to numb letting sorrow's ice fill my chest
to save me from the torturous ways of living life with a soul of unrest

Peace comes to me now for love there is no cure
but emotions I can hide away simply locking their iron door

So bare your lustrous body and join me in the dance
fulfilling the primal needs without the trappings of romance

Come willingly and knowing that it's all just fun and games
for I'll not linger within your grasp to see the light of day

Restless Sighs
Written August 6, 2005

Sapphires crave acceptance
of society's approval
contentment overshadowing
the spirits longing to mate
with a soul intertwined

So moonlit serenades
whisper upon deaf ears
lost in denial
of the perfect package
wrapped in love's disguise

And lonely hearts merely beat
with shallow restless sighs

Vampire Revelation
Written April 16, 2004

You sought to covet the great divine of my shadows
yet the fear of my light was forsaken by your arrogance
though nocturnal, does God's light not shine upon me
I am but a beast amongst the food chain, the same as you
as cattle is to your stomach, so your blood shall be to mine
I am the closest to god that shall ever be
for on the very essence of his creations I dine

Like an angel I walk, watching the world change
humanity disappearing behind soulless eyes
my beauty bewitching, until you want to be me
stalking me on the chance that I may take your life
shudder in my embrace and gaze into my eyes
stare into the history of the human race and tell me
do you really want to live for all time

Bewitched Again
Written April 2004

I was a vision to behold, a power beyond measure
spiritually enlightened, a healer to be treasured

The elements at my fingertips, the Goddess blessing me each day
then I ran across your path and to you my heart, I gave

I opened my wings wide asking you to stare into my soul
revealing the truth of me so I could be accepted as whole

Gazing upon me with emerald eyes, a tear streaming down your face
you swore to me and promised to never try to replace my faith

Bliss you brought into my world, filling my days with love and laughter
but the joke was on me really, it was only my power you were after

And though I raged in your deception as my eyes refused to see
I swallowed the curse from my lips wishing only for you to be happy

Now you try returning to my life to bring me back into your arms
I swear to you this night, my love, flee from me, before I do you harm

For once again I am a vision to behold, a power beyond measure
spiritually enlightened, a healer to be treasured

The elements at my fingertips, the Goddess blessing me each day
and to protect myself from your grip, our love, I've already cast away

Purging Denied
Written May 2004

Upon a shattered wall I sat
screaming to the raging wind
Releasing the misery inside from
the stale taste of your love
As the stones gouged my flesh
your face haunted my eyes

And so it came, pure blood
lost in hollow victory of a broken heart
Winds grazing the cheek
where lips should have been
Reminding my soul of your memories
the very essence of my torment

Discarded Lover's Insomnia
Written September 1998

Many times I've tossed and turned
waiting for sleep to claim my weary soul
but naught is the blessing to soothe away
the pain that holds my heart captured so
I fight myself for a shred of peace
to trick my mind to empty into the night
but your face appears as my thoughts clear
and within my mind, there begins a new fight
oh, disappear love that haunts me so
let your talons relinquish their grip
for you alone can set me free
from the purgatory I reside within

Resurrection from Sorrow's Tomb
Written April 2004

Sounds long ago were drowned by tears
washing away the light that shone
through eyes of many lives gone by
memories awakened to be denied
by words of love from a heart of stone

Smiling and laughing, though dying
I suffered where none could see
loneliness long surpassed passion
soul shrouded as my limbs froze
heartbreak and pain, a faded misery

I wrapped myself within the essence
of the weavings of a mastered mind
a web spun golden, turned to dust
encased like ancient treasure
waiting to be found, lost in time

And then Isis came in splendor
golden wings wrapping me tight
whispering words into my ear
finger tips then touched me gently
wiping dust from my steely eyes

She unwrapped my layers one by one
as within the coma of silence I slept
a secret, hidden below the surface
immune to the call of the blazing sun
reaching deep into the earth's depth

My daughter, you shall rise again
and take your place, here at my side
empowered with my healing grace
quickened, strong of heart and mind
I resurrect you from this dismal guise

And as my aura glowed purple and gold
upon her gilded wings, I arose from the tomb
the priestess, revived from age old vows
stepping into the light of Amun-Ra
once again with the mysteries, in tuned

179

Sacred Night
Written May 2005

As the moon kisses the mountains
I stand solid against the rocks
awaiting the coming of her splendor
music wafting through the air

My arms outstretched I call upon the mother
the inner circle dancing and chanting
drawing and stirring energies
as the outer watches in anticipation

The ancients guard me as I trance
my gown, scarves of white and gold
billowing in the winds as my body sways
the quickening before her arrival thrilling me

Indigo fires fill my mind as I shiver
golden light filtering through my body
she eases into me like electric pulses
looking through my eyes to her children

Completely aware that I am not myself
but a vessel housing the Goddess
as she wanders around slowly
her song flowing from my silken lips

I glow with the essence of her energies
as they move throughout my body and soul
her presence is a blessing to all that view
and all that come to gaze upon her light

Her arms, my arms, reach to take the wounded
the sick, the weak and diseased within them
blessing them with her healing voice and touch
my consciousness relinquishing to her power

Awakening to the breeze completely chilling me
I look down at my glowing body, covered in sweat
and then out amongst the faces of the cured
watching as they smile upon the full moon light

I do not recall the ancients taking their leave
or the tongues spoken throughout the rite
but I know I've done as I was meant to do
as i walk empowered into the dead of night

Akasha's Plea
Written May 15, 2004

Come ride the waves of indigo fire
raining cascades of eternal light
visit me within your mind, embrace me
my existence forged the Tree of Life

I am the Mother of Mother Nature
the one who bore Father Time
born from them were the elements
that created your world and human kind

From Air, Fire, Water and Earth
comes the plants and food you eat
the trees that clean all that you poison
so that you can live and breathe

They give to you creatures of wonder
essences of flowers, the breeze in the air
the fire to warm your chilling bones
water to drink, bathe and wash your hair

Feeding all that you have forsaken
their energies try to sustain your world
as you destroy what was given to you
they cry for help to keep life preserved

Won't you wipe away my tears
for I am grieving for each of you
as the greenery turns to dying dust
and their elements are misused

Come back into the folds of nature
for their energies have never left you
and upon my wings of hope you'll rise
as the earth heals from it's abuse

Pain Killers & Wine
Written April 2001

Champagne lilies
and formaldehyde dreams
locked together
in a world of deceit

Love dripping like honey
from rose colored lips
of a soul with no depth
only promises adrift

In a sea of woes
trust was gained
with a backward glance
finally sealing fate

Eyes tightly shut
arms opened wide
poised for a kiss
once again denied

Just a glimpse of life
facing the blackened knife
of a fancy date
with pain killers and wine

My Prayer (The Chant)
Written December 20, 2002

Ancient powers stir and grow
lightness and dark , above and below
Lift the veil and bridge the worlds
open the channels let my heart be heard

Raise me gently so I can fly
to my secret place on the other side
In the realm where I'm at peace
free me of emotions within serenity

Drifting to Candy Land
Written December 5, 2002

Follow me, I'm drifting to a place I can't resist
with marmalade flowers and cotton candy mist
Unicorns are playing by a chocolate filled stream
as leprechauns dance on clouds of whipped cream

See the fairy over there resting on a licorice twist
winding tightly through trees of the lollipop forest
Dragons roast marshmallows on graham cracker crust
as elves bring chocolate and share S'mores with us

Mermaids are singing near the butterscotch falls
I start to drift deeper as the winged horse talks
He tells me great stories of ice cream slopes
where we can slide right down on banana boats

It's raining rainbow sprinkles so I lean back to watch
resting against the sweetness of a purple gum drop
I stare into the sky watching striped starlight mints
pondering softly to myself on this wonder I'm in

And as I sit up slowly, wondering what's going on
I get a weighted realization I must have dozed off
Kids are giggling as they pounce down upon me
What a fine day it is, to fall asleep beneath a tree

Creatures of the Night
Written December 15, 2002

Mystery of mysteries
hidden for all time
lurking in the darkness
watching all of mankind

They are the breeze at night
the chill on the air
the sufferers, the sinners
the evil things beware

They follow you at random
they frighten with great skill
you are forever the victims
as they stalk and kill

The choice is not their own
for they know no other way
but should you encounter them
with your life you'll surely pay

Watch your back and search
for the fierce eyes that glow
and veer far from the creature
with the skin as white as snow

They travel through our world
not knowing how or why
only that they live forever
as creatures of the night

Spell Bound
December 18, 2002

Light glowing
where you thought none
colors swirl
the darkness fades
as the voice calls your name

Moving in a trance
you follow
Not knowing where you go
you sense the presence
of the unknown

Tickles upon your face
a breeze where there is none
steadily flowing forth
upon a rainbow
that was spun

Reaching out your hand
it closes on air
yet the coolness
spreads
your feet are bare

Spiraling in the mist
through deep indigo
weightless
timeless
no thoughts of your own

Where are you now
where should you go
you've no idea
fearless yet lost
spell bound you go

Meet Me At The End Of The World
Written December 26, 2002

You know who you are , I know this you'll see
I'll be waiting out here at our place by the sea
Just like from the time the thunderstorm came
we stood at the railing and called the gods name

The storm is brewing thunder at a roar
winds gusting me backwards my dress is torn
My heads flung back at the winds request
spray from the ocean hits me like a caress

Barefooted and worn, hungry and used
I wait for you now, for you are my muse
My thoughts, my soul, my mysteries so deep
the child within that I cannot defeat

I stand here alone at the end of the pier
crying for you, hoping you'll hear
Violated and broke, defiled and bruised
I know it's not my fault but I've been so abused

Come claim me once more, I stand here for you
give me the strength let my power shine through
I'm here in the darkness peering into the abyss
at our end of the world just like when we were kids

Dragon's Revenge
Written January 6, 2003

Dragons of fire, dragons galore
I conjure you up to even the score
Show no mercy on this vengeful flight
Seek out the injustice and make it right

Spread your wings, breathe your fire
haunt the dreams of those you desire
Move swift as wind through the dead of night
use your cloak of illusions amongst daylight

Seek out those that you do not believe
those who befriended only to deceive
Entangle them in their own sordid lies
let them rot and ignore their cries

Make haste with your vengeance
My most loyal companions and friends
They brought the war with their games
And now, now their reigns at an end

Comfort's Charade
Written March 29, 2006

Sorrow begotten delight, such a bittersweet effect
dowsed in false whispers of passion's liquored sweat

Ashen tears and ruby lips caress tangled ivory limbs
forging licorice life lines against soiled cotton linens

Faded whims of forest hues deny an abyss as it creeps
upon broken party favors as oblivious bodies sleep

A mad hatter's charade of love lost and pain's reign
proving that through it all life's antiquities never fade

187

Forgotten Ways
Written January 13, 1998

I stand alone, invisible in the presence of your divine light
within a realm once adored to gain knowledge and insight
Though the followers are gone, from this world they must hide
they seek your help and guidance, as their spirits slowly die

We are shunned from the world, for we are indeed feared
they claim we worship the devil with these words, my heart tears
They know not the beauty of what we do truly believe
their ignorance causes fears from a church who deceives

They've taken our symbols of protection and love
neglecting to remember their religion was once a part of
They've taken our Gods and shunned them as well
The Horned One, made a devil who would burn them in hell

Casting aside the old ways for what they claim is new
forgetting the earth's plants and all the things they can do
Fighting with each other, killing each other in God's name
breaking their own commandments, harboring no shame

I think I shall never understand why to them the highest powers
must be worshipped in a way that makes life seem so sour
In their ignorance they do not realize universal powers are the same
it doesn't matter what they call you, your form comes in all names

As I stand here alone, invisible in the presence this night
I ask you to bring peace to all so we may live and not fight
Though your followers are gone from this place, this home
They await your splendor to show them, they are not alone

Deceptive Climax
August 18, 2006

No, they wouldn't know me now

Poised confident, my hair down
and life's twinkle fueling my eyes
casting bold glances of seduction
across marble slabs of innocence

Vain, they'd be coaxing lust
with smooth deliverance to coy charms
lost in the desperation of whims
seeking to mesh with feigned desire

Willingly trapped in a web of fantasia
we'd twirl against shimmers of ebony
caressing silver sequins of starlight
heated flesh, teasing silken measures

Screaming souls muffled against lips
full of venom, savoring their moment
justified by a whore labeled heart
siphoning the power of love scorned
recognition denied by death's door

Breathing Life
Written November 27, 2005

Serenity come to claim me for you're all that I have left
Love is gone and passion flown but I still draw life's breath

I feel my heart beat steady as life pours into my lungs
Willing me to wake each day and without love, move on

Taking away the sorrow light replacing all the pain
With visions of indigo hues to pass my days away

And with every dawn I'll smile knowing each day starts anew
Bringing hope for all that's lost as sun kisses the morning dew

Spell of Winter
Written November 19, 2005

Holly berries lay glistening, upon bare branches
beneath perfect bulbs of ice, towards the sun
how enchanted I stood, before life's miracle
witnessing Autumn preserved by Winter's hand

My every breath, a plume of eternal mist
against the haze of reality, coming for an embrace
bare feet lost in the chill of crisp sleet, mesmerized
as the wind's wisps of seduction claimed my heart

And there I gazed upon the miracle of divinity
clutching the reins of our very existence, in splendor
refusing to allow the stagnation of the universe
forcing nature itself to take a rest from fertilization

Thoughts no longer a plague, but a realization
that rebirth is the sheer power, everlasting energy
to sustain the aftermath of disasters and cruelties
hibernating, secretly rejuvenating in essence

Snowflakes slowly begin to fall, each so cleverly unique
as to hide their tiny, opaque forms from prying eyes
providing a hazy blanket of perfection to grace us
as the eyesore of barren land, heals in silence

Closing my eyes I partake of the euphoria, never hidden
merely cast aside by the mundane tides of the world
and move to the whimsical music, drifting to my ears
knowing this spell of winter, I've never before heard

Prelude of the Succubus
Written July 21, 2005

Pristine beguiles elude animosity
sacrificed in throes of formaldehyde dreams
wasting chains of metamorphosis
against an ashen face, diamond cracked
in the aftermath of amour
adhering lust's shadows in satin sheets
upon the nemesis of phantasm

Escapism supreme, reigns
charcoal lined eyes, etched onyx
wielding seduction's tasteless ruin
virginity's nemesis strangled in venom
leaving welts upon crimson lips smiling
opaque aftertaste, creamed passion
clawing destruction, pleasuring pain

Stark denial speaks through silver
glares of dreams dissipated, lurk
menace remaining solid in life's fortitude
reveling in whims of desolate behavior
insurrection exudes whiskey's stale scent
amber courage of the predator, lingering
against silken skin like French perfume

Lucid bodies taunt the senses
sharpening the claws of demonic play
black leather covering the vessel's form
sheer desire blazing a pointed tongue
against a coward's fear, mercilessly
traversing the bliss of sleep, violating
innocence unspoiled by rapture's use
she devours you

Aware
Written July 1998

Close your eyes

Relax with me

Beyond the dreams
to the silence beyond all that you know

Here there is no time
There is no pain

Here is beyond all that is
beyond what ever shall be

Infinite wisdom staring at you
waiting to be heard

Beckoning

Colors fly free in your mind
it's left your earthly body

Running free in the ethers
taking knowledge in

Freeing you from that which binds
the fears that cling

Relax as the pictures form
visions floating your way

Like a movie it rolls
the voices come

You hear

You seek

You are

AWARE

I Could, But I Can't

Written July 10, 2005

Lingering, I could fall
but I can't...

Fall into the enchantment of pain
that your soul somehow makes content

You see me clearly, knowing my torment
The only luxury I contain

But I can't fall...

Letting my heart melt against your musky scent
knowing my heart, you'd tame

I won't lie and say the thought doesn't cross my mind
or that I wouldn't want to entertain the desire sometime

But I just can't fall...

I'm not sure I can take it again
the hellish struggle of not wanting to want

Though if I could, I would
if only to hold you in my arms, just once

But I can't fall in love
So don't look at me that way

This heart closed long ago
When sorrow cultivated from love's seed
suffocated into ashes, the ashes that were me

Ardor's Daze
Written July 19, 2005

Glances
Flirtations
Craving flesh

Touching lips
Moving mouths
Probing Tongues

Roaming hands
Tangled bodies
Quenching Lust

Blissful sleep
Shameful wake
Lonely daze

All for one moment
of another's willing embrace

Humdrum of Life
Written December 31, 2002

Sands of time, we work against
with no real knowledge of what comes to pass
Most of us locked away in our conscious mind
lost in ignorance in this place and time

Dwelling each day looking for more
having no idea what our minds store
Subconsciously we know we hold the key
to open our mind and set ourselves free

Yet most choose the bliss of living our lives
in the chaos at hand, while within we hide
Is it the fear of what's out there unknown
or have we lost touch with our very soul

194

Evaluating You
Written August 1, 2005

Don't speak a word ~ Just let me hear
Don't show yourself ~ Just let me see
Don't touch me ~ Just let me feel
Please stay where you are
I'll know if you are real

Emotional Overload
Written July 11, 2005

Focus didn't grace today, not in the slightest way
it kept me lost and bound quite unable to ground

You were etched in mind never letting it unwind
my torment slowly eased creating aches unappeased

Blue orbs mingled in lashes upon my heart, leaving slashes
bleeding the pain from my soul with dreams of again being whole

Fantasy reigned within visions of emotion's sacred provisions
as my body lusted for arms that would keep me from harm

Passion stirred as I blushed, energy's euphoria rushed
claiming senses long dead imagining you in my bed

Logic fought with illusions of growing desires infusions
until I sat down and cried realizing my heart never died

Now I'm lost in great waves wondering what brought the blaze
that sparked long dead fires beneath walls built from liars

My spirit merely longs to be free but I keep seeing images of me
hoping to lay contently embraced waking up only feeling disgraced

Saving Face
Written July 13, 2005

Chimera locked phantasm
stained spider's eyes
etched in tears
against denial's silken cheeks

Discarded remnants
of nocturnal delights
wavering senses of waste
in passion's wake

Agitation adds to hysteria
seeking absolution
in freedom denied
at the hands of L'oreal

Frantic fingers
seeking vanity's saving maneuver
ransack unfamiliar drawers
yielding only broken nails

Desolate, on a porcelain throne
victory drifts through calm winds
carrying scents of aloe
breathing in the night

Glass panes lifted
reveals tentacles of redemption
awaiting shaky hands
to squeeze their full essence

Gel embraces cotton
slowly soothing away disgrace
freeing a smile to welcome
awaiting eyes of blue

As apologies filter
through a closed door

Encircled Karma
Written July 15, 2005

A Vision of Power
Untainted or jaded stands spiritually complete
full of confidence and love reaching to those in need

A Tattered Heart
Mourning love, how sheik in denials aftermath
desolate feelings inhibiting hysteria's lecherous path

A Smiling Face
Conjured illusions of friendship warmth pretending resurrection
within ringlets of smoke and undying affections

A Lonely Heart
Dulled enlightened eyes under dismal soul's embrace
seeking absolution of fault in euphoria misplaced

A Serpent's Shadow
Torments a weary mind opening doors to hidden lust
un-denied, but savoring the trusting hand of true love

A Shattered Delusion
Encumbers rays of hope as embers of fire lick ice
spurring a heart lost in fantasy to give another chance to life

A Raging Witch Emerges
Defying violation of solitude shards rising like silver blades
riding the crest of enchantments intoning within astral waves

A Reckoning
Manifests upon violators heads as their world comes tumbling down
into self wrought hell of demon's rings cries of mercy rise without a sound

A Vision of Power
Tainted and slightly jaded stands, almost spiritually complete
full of confidence, seeking love reaching to those in need

Marlboro Reds and Amber Eyes
Written July 15, 2005

Dreams disrupted
Invaded by lingering scents
Burnt ash riding cool winds
Assaulting nostrils almost sensually
In anticipation, I await his touch

Softly crushed
embers die against glass
as he exhales a Marlboro red
body weight indenting teal sheets
a sure signal he wants me

Callused fingers roam softly
over long legs that feign sleep
as the mind transfixes upon sensations
rising steadily as they glide
towards territory well known

A smile hiding in feathered bliss
knows soon his arms will claim me
rolling me over to gaze in amber eyes
his heat rising against my back
answering seductive hips

Sleek maneuvers position me
with the grace of a panther stalking prey
as he shares his cigarette's essence
with full lips that greedily accept
the offering of passion's reign

Riding euphoria, he takes me
quivering complete in lust's caress
musky scents chasing smoke away
leaving sighs rising on cool winds
to greet the dawn of a new day

Pucha-Pot Saturn's Whore *(Patchouli)*
Written July 29, 2005

Saturn's whore assaults my senses
Catastrophic waves of sinus hell turning to
prime time upheaval in a small dimly lit room

Cascading pheromones, lost in denial reach
gripping waves of hope presented via earth
personified in amber mist

Oblivious to death, purple haze of the seventies
haunt synthetic revolutions, defying toilette water
deemed body nectar by Calvin Klien

Embodied suffering spurs demonic frenzy
in self preservation voiced thoughts run amuck
slicing confidence into tissue paper wisps

Tactless honesty overwhelms a wounded heart
as tongued kisses seek violation of silken lips
meeting disdain upon nostril breezes

Enlightened with reality patchouli's scent
meets bubbles' erasure, embarrassment craving rectification
as freshly washed flesh beams a wanton glance

Yielding only witch cackles sung like chants of jest
"Money, lust and fertility from the Pucha-Pot does seep
within a charm, not on the skin, its passionate power shall keep"

Saturn's whore meet the porcelain God
a coward of justice, dying untamed laughter its bane
passion's only memory relinquished to chocolate mousse

Mind Warrior Prophecy
Written July 30, 2002

Adorned in black, we walk
absorbing universal light
between the realms of worlds
as we prepare to fight

Within a war, millenniums old
seeking to change healing shifts
from those that would destroy
the very world we live within

I seek you now, the kindred
to take up arms, side by side
with the elements behind us
guiding us to do what's right

Listen intently to the earth
hear the anger you can't see
the sorrow of the cleansing
that has finally come to be

Storms will bring destruction
in the wake of it's desire
waves churning with animosity
crashing beneath skies of fire

Hearken to the Angel's voices
for their time has come to rage
upon the narrow minded
through floods, winds and rains

Behind hallow masks of victory
our enemies shall once again fall
as upon sacred ground, we'll stand
continuing to answer Divinity's call

Absolution does not come
for those that harm the innocent
no being shall stand in pity
of their wounded souls repent

Among the calming of the storm
our world shall forever shine
peace freeing us once again
to live without fear in our lives

The Healing
Written July 31, 2005

Beneath the call of the moon
adorned in nature's clothes
with arms outstretch, I reel
as energies ebb and flow

Embraced by divinity, I call
upon the winds of change
manifesting desires intoned
as magical energies vibrate

Bare feet seemingly weightless
as I stare into other realms
the Goddess answering my call
lifting me up beyond the veil

Euphoric sensations claim me
thoughts and visions unite
pages of Akashic records turn
as healing commences this night

Universal light, blazing blue
pure of essence fills my being
dis-ease forming blackened streams
moving away from my physical body

Awakening upon a bed of earth
I arise, quickened with life
confirmation of an illness gone
taken away by Divinity's Light

I Don't Want You
Written August 1, 2005

Years, I've waited to be held
Held in arms through the nights
nights filled with passion
Passion turning to love
love to share my life

I don't want you!

Phantom hands touching
touching sensual places
places igniting desires
desires to be held in arms
arms that hold me tightly

No, I don't want you!

You are worse than my life
life spent seeking love
love within warm bodies
bodies that always left
left before the sun ever rose

I definitely don't want you!

Taunting dreams of longing
longing for a life of love
love filled with passion
passion that lingers
lingers to be with me

I shall never want you!

You are the loneliness
I've always awoken to

Washing Away the Lady

Written August 1, 2001

I stand naked in the sunset
water trickling down my chest
rainbows over head
stones caressing my back

Dreaming of a memory
as I wash away the sins
of a love that left me tainted
with the blood of my hearts bliss

Tears stream from my eyes
salty taste upon my lips
as my hands roam down my body
washing away the debris

Clinging to the shadows
of the spell once cast
to free my soul from your strings
and give my mind a needed rest

And the realization comes to me
of just what it is I am
I'm your pleasure
I'm your whore

The woman lying in your bed
to use as you will
because it's all that I know
and all I've ever been

So I wash your love away
from my long term fantasy
and I walk along the banks
for a new man to see

I've got what he wants
and I know the ways
to pleasure him, like you
I'm strong and love's dream...
has finally faded away

Destiny's Path
Written August 2001

Could you live within my fantasy
amongst the flowers and trees
deep in the forest with me alone
far away from the big cities

Would you walk with me
as I venture to my sacred land
Watching the enchantments
that dwell outside the world of man

Is your mind as open as you say
do you really understand me
or deep inside does it worry you
that I may suffer from insanity

To come into my world
you must give me your trust
to stay within my life
you must offer me true love

I dwell within the mysteries
a realm of knowledge and peace
once you cross the threshold
you may never leave

So I ask you again, my love
could you live within my fantasy
the choice is yours to make
take your time, choose wisely

For we have eternity

Oraculum
Written August 2001

Lacquered in perfection's mask
I gaze upon the unforeseen
A tainted glimpse of shadow's breath
that taunts me wake and sleep

Blood flows as charcoal swirls
visions strong behind closed eyes
Alabaster pages once left blank
slowly begin to come to life

Fate circles as it deals it's hand
leaving nothing left unseen
Suspending me in a neon shroud
of what I know shall never be

Antiquated Portals
Written August 2005

Unique hauntings remain immortalized
within colored hues or black and white

Treasures seeking resurrection of the soul
through eyes blind to secrets unrevealed

Brush stroked images or captured frames
taunt the restless as well as the pristine

While Captivation conjures a lingering aftermath
opening doorways to time that beckon the mind

Delving there in silence visions speak words unsaid
like wind chime tunes playing the key of life

Antiquated portals open the ebb and flow of emotion
trying to decipher a maze left open for interpretation

And there we find the magic a moment frozen in time
striving to move strangers into an intimacy
that speaks a thousand words, yet unheard

Snuffing the Light
Written August 5, 2005

Mankind, plagued
lost in shadows of denial
mundanely tainted
third eye blind

Armed silhouettes
a demon's disguise
harboring seeds of chaos
waiting to rise

Silver phantasm
interlace woes
implanting souls
with birth's illusion

Psyches bare
welcoming their chaos
reaping shadows
upon rebirth's confusion

Evil's laughter reigns
destruction of quaint days
the world falling apart
in a blackened haze

Sublime delusion
all that remains
of a walking corpse
living life untamed

Iris of the Mind's Eye
Written August 2005

Hallowed, they lie
against the balance of time
transfixed within a sphere
representing the world's eye

Serenity, the angel
wrapped in pristine silk
entwined with chaos
the reaper of sorrow's guilt

In dreams they encumber
the edge of lost reality
awake they exhibit
a world seeking to dream

Together for eternity
their existence, sweetly sublime
retaining synchronicity
within the world's trouble mind

Yin & Yang
Written August 2005

Non-discriminative powers born of one divine source
A trickle of God's two hands balancing universal life force

The perfection of all remains yet always warring within
spiraling the light of lights beneath the shadows of sin

Doorways of spirituality awaiting our choice to be cast
as our lessons here on earth fight sands of time's hourglass

Femininity, masculinity harboring both good and evil
seeking enlightenment of the soul within the world's prime upheaval

Uninhibited against ourselves we dance in duality as we strain
each personally responsible for the balance of yin and yang

Dragon's Breath
Written August 2005

Dragon's eyes gleam blood fire

Liquefied molten streams kill disdain
cementing chaos against the earth
hardening to diamond edges
cutting tethers long denying spiritual rebirth

Reclaiming the breath of life

His Song
Written August 2005

Sweet mournful songs carry upon the dying winds
through corridors of the world that we both once lived within
And though I fight to see you and feel one last embrace
I know you're gone forever, yet I long to touch your face

I mourn the way you touched me with your body, heart and soul
your laugh, your wit, your tenderness were the things that made me whole
I know I should not cling to us and release you from my mind
but my heart still hears your song like you're with me all the time

Sandman Stalking
Written October 2003

To the nightmares that come while we're awake,
never should we dwell or leave to hate
but take our minds to deeper sands
forgetting the pawn that tipped our hand

For should the nightmare become real
our world shall crumble at the turn of the wheel
manifestations will come, destruction in its wake
and become the deliverer that sealed our fate

Empty Mirror Screams
Written March 2003

Glaciers melt to ice water chasing the boiling blood in my veins
reminding me of the heartache your love causes me each day

As I cry out, I long to flea and free myself from your grip
I know without you my soul would die an even more agonizing death

So touch me with your blade of chaos ruin me with your everlasting lies
I shall be here for you forever in the shadows with closed eyes

As sparrows taint the shattered glass upon the bed in which we laid
crimson drops drip from the rose outside my window pane

Oblivious
Written August 2005

Time cares not to worry
its passing isn't grave
unbending to whims of man
often spiritually depraved

Glowing embers silently drift
the essences of past lives
as they ride upon naked wind
waiting to be realized

Awakening deeper images
to what reality can't see
beyond the gates of heaven
only mind and souls are key

Oblivious to it all, we stare
through shallow hearts and eyes
ignorance wasting who we truly are
brilliance lost in human guise

209

Soul Healer
Written August 1999

Between the worlds, I stand emerging to new heights
melding with the energies of the supreme divine

Invincible to destruction both shadow and light
filled with the quickening of the elements combined

All and no-thing, complete, empowered within serenity
basking in the glory of life and the many facets of me

An obelisk, a shining beacon, a vessel of divinity's energies
guiding the weary home within the shift of natural healing

Sacred Resurrection
Written August 2005

Mystic fog encumbers lovers revealing nothing to the world
as passion ignites in sacred rite consummating divine rebirth

Frenzied lust of torch light songs master chants against their moans
transcending them beyond the realm mundane reality, merely shadows

Smoldering incense, musky essence mingle in ties that eternally bind
as the priestess takes the priest into the hollow of her gripping tides

Soaring upon crests of divinity's light, pentacles blaze protective shrouds
seed sown in an enlightened womb, life force renewed in orgasmic bounds

The Goddess smiles, seductively sated, the God claims his bride once more
for within their coupling upon our earth, primal balance is again restored

Morning Mantra
Written 1998

Morning wakes me with its song
enchanting the dance within me
as I gaze upon the light of lights
past the veil of earth's reality

And to the Great Mother, I chant
my arms poised for her embrace
renewing vows of everlasting faith
within dawn's brilliant rays

"Great Mother of the All
I call to you this hour
to bless me in your light
and fill me with your power

Great Mother of the Earth
heal my wounds, set me free
empower me with knowledge
grant me prosperity and stability

Great Mother of the Sky
may you always light my way
bestowing me with wisdom
so in this life I truly see

Great Mother of Eternal Fire
fill me with courage and strength
quicken me with your passions
keep the warrior within me safe

Great Mother of Healing Springs
cleanse me within your falls
wash away that which binds
freeing my energy flow

And to your light, I shall be true
following your ways with honor
upon the infinite sands of time
your faithful, loving daughter"

Her power fills my essence
my spirit prepared to face the day
I move within the world
full of her divine grace

Society's Mannequins
Written June 2004

Gilded they stand
blending in the game
of life on the run
and people full of shame

No ethics left to pass
to generations in need
for they've lost their
souls to society's pleas

Blended as though molded
into stone corners and halls
silently wishing to be different
but they've not got the balls

They hide, sublime
never willing to fight
for the individuality
that brings color to life

Laughter never cracking
gold streams of Lamay
seething to their flesh
even in winter's days

Robotic they roam
under the watchful eyes
of hypocrisy turn amuck
in a world gone awry

Mannequins 'til the end
plastic smiles, dim minds
but not me, I'm walking
in kaleidoscope skies

Above new world order
beyond shallow schemes
I refuse to be tethered
for I am indigo dreams

Open Field
Written October 8, 2005

Fragrant blossoms reach towards amber rays
releasing joy's fragrance within the heaven of our reality

Star Glide
Written September 2005

Black wings call my fancy taking me beyond the gate
past lights of eternal bliss into the mysteries that await

Scales rest between my thighs as I hold tight to the reigns
of a dragon, lost in flight beneath the ethers, as they sing

Barley Moon Ritual
Written September 2005

Arms outstretched as spiraling energies rise
we embrace the light filtered through azure skies

Skyclad we stand, Barley gracing our sight
we chant in tune to the call of the night

Silvery rays caress words of enchanted lips
as incense smolders dance moving our hips

In celebration, we honor the harvest at hand
with ritual blessings for the gifts of the land

Together in unison children of the earth
drawing down the moon for the soil's rebirth

Scar Dust
Written September 22, 2005

Communication falters
ebbing in silence
while lying glances
deny smiles
awaiting consummation
of acceptance
lost in shadows
of contempt

Unspoken promises
of friendship die
like embers against ice
etching scars
of loneliness
into a jaded heart
that only desired
a human touch

Passion numbs
accompanying pain
in an embrace
solidifying a promise
made upon dying winds
until she fades
like a withered rose
into indigo haze

Emerging powerfully hollow
immune to love's lust

Shangri-la
Written October 10, 2005

There is a place where the beauty of your heart
is never overshadowed by the evil of your smile
It is a place of enchantment, peace and serenity
Known to all that care to glimpse into its realm

It is a world owned by no one, yet inhabited by many
filled with your wildest dreams and most beautiful fantasies
It is a haven for the weak, the unwanted and the maimed
It is home of the healers, the seekers and the enlightened

All may enter here, if they are pure of mind
purity of heart follows and the songs of souls unsung
bellow out amongst the trees and are carried on the winds
for all that care to hear its rhythm and dance

There is no fear here, no hatred or disgust
It holds none of society's labels or petty innuendos
But sees us all as equals, dwelling side by side
healing one another as all heart and spirits shine

It is the paradise we all long for at the core of our being
A place for us to roam in perfect harmony, waiting patiently
For you to unlock its silvery gates and step inside
Need the key? Simply open your mind

Love's Embrace
Written October 25, 2005

Encircled within love's embrace
we are separate souls
bound as one

Flawed and helpless
to the sighs of our desire
and the comfort of our hearts

Fierce and strong
against all that would come
to separate our union

Different from each other
and yet the same
in so many ways

Our perfection is the balance
of the beauty of our light
and the sorrow of our darkness

Sometimes we falter
against the currents of life
and the distance of hope

But some how, some way
fate pulls us back into a trust of love
everlasting and ever-changing

Into the flawed perfection of "us"
and there we shall be as we are
as we always should be

Encircled in love's embrace

The Masterpiece of You
Written September 10, 2004

Have you ever seen inside you?
I mean really delved in deep
to those parts hidden, locked away
lying dormant, beyond the door
to all the secrets inside you keep

To the part of you that is adored
by true friends and family
past the flesh, beyond the blood
through the mask you wear
shattering illusion's serendipity

Without blind eyes or a closed mind
beyond emotion's iron door
traveling through the heart
into the glowing encasement
of your very deep, old soul

Have you ever seen inside you?
past the veils we see right through
beyond the pain of childhood
to the courage underneath
opening the door to the real you

Into the eyes in the mirror
where the light inside you keeps
the shadows from taking away
all the things that you possess
that make you truly unique

My friend, I look inside of you
and see all the rainbows brilliant hues
from the darkest to the lightest streaks
each one a swirling enigma
painting the masterpiece of you

And I wonder, do you see them to?

Wasted Immortality
Written November 6, 2005

Chimera shatters serene thoughts
embraced in chains, I must confide
demons passed to chaotic ends
leaving immortality, my surprise

Winds yield a wicked frostbite
flesh sheering in their caress
blind and numb, I seek forgiveness
yet feel nothing but discontent

Empires forged in desolate waste
tame the ramblings of my mind
bones of kin, mere scattered remnants
once contained my zest for life

Greed of blood lust hunger
consumed a world of smiling faces
laughter echoes empty halls
I rot barren, never sated

Slowly, cruel sands of time
grind against my marrowed bones
as my essence joins the winds
following my flesh to realms unknown

Until the bitter end, I wait
wondering if the mind will fade away
as my crystalline essence flows free
seeking blood, with nothing to sustain

Hibernating Mind Threads
Written November 6, 2005

As through her body, the Goddess Shines

Enchantments become a prison
womanly essences run astray
beneath the painful knowledge
that once again she's betrayed

Betrayed by lust enraptured
with energies long kept dormant
beneath the withered heart
iced over from years of torment

Torment wielded like a weapon
against a motherhood of dreams
a child's laughter dead in the womb
beneath a father's anger, released

Released upon nature's freak
not good enough to bear his seed
promises spoken in love, mere lies
to sate the desire of manly needs

Needs he loved, spread wild fires
through his loins, her energy he craved
claiming bewitched in society's face
he walks smugly thinking he's safe

Safe to play the field, a murderer
killer of wombs, hearts and minds
But vengeance comes to the innocent
and sorrow heals, in its own time

As through her body, the Goddess Shines

Delirium at Dawn
Written December 27, 2005

Weary bones elude dawn's silence
as the soul sighs its body's release
within impassioned throes of ecstasy
 beneath the hands of phantom heat

Glimpsing melancholy silhouettes
transgressions plummet lost lives
torments and victories revealed
traces of imperfection, taste sublime

Facets of self denial, dance in dreams
integration of personalities subtly wake
serenity's light taunts secret seductions
casting muted tones of spiritual embrace

Euphoria claims those lucid moments
reigning upon edges of fitful sleep
a mind tease of fascination, embedded
against the coolness of satin sheets

Weary bones elude dawn's silence
as the soul sighs its body's release
within impassioned throes of ecstasy
beneath the hands of phantom heat

Awaiting Unity of Minds
Written March 1, 2006

Colored energies collide
phantoms of earth, in flesh
seeking unity while imprisoned
within society's stale breath

And I wonder, how I wonder
what miracles I shall see
as I float upon the essence
of the pollen of the trees

Winter's grasp has ebbed
spring flowing into life
calling my spirit home
brothers and sisters at my side

And I wonder, how I wonder
what miracles I shall see
when last the sun rise touches
the horizon laid before me

Dancing in the moonlight
the raven's call echoes there
embraces come quite random
bringing love, we all can share

And I wonder, how I wonder
how loneliness can reign
within the hearts of children
beating against broken dreams

All the world sparkles
and yet so many refuse to see
that nature lives inside us
breathing with every plant and tree

And here I wonder, yes I wonder
as I meld within soils of the earth
how long shall it take for humanity
to grasp the reality of rebirth

A Woman Renewed
Written April 6, 2006

Reflections taunt shadows of youth
denied by society's demand to grow
yet here I am, within a fantasy
before a silent silver window

Orbs of life, gleam as if all knowing
displaying a part of myself, long denied
inner whispers encourage the woman I am
with shadows of the one I left behind

A moment of resurrection, enjoyed
sparking sensuality with shaded hues
cosmetic rituals empower the mind
with dreams of flesh again renewed

Transformed, a humble beauty
confident again in silken threads
twirls eagerly within the splendor
of masked personas that lie ahead

Lost in Passion's Throes
Written April 6, 2006

Shuddering, I lay lost in passion's throes
swirling in waves of memories denying the waking world

Silken caresses linger like steadily heated flames
between sheets of crimson silk entwined between my legs

My body writhes seductively within the scents of lovers gone
claiming sanctity within a world holding only heartbreaking chaos

Here euphoria, my lucid drug, claims the sorrow, I held at bay
for within this realm of pleasure there is no shadows of my pain

Back to My Realm
Written January 2003

I wandered to your world
I tried to live your ways
but my soul cried out to me
and my heart broke everyday

They yearned for the knowledge
reaching for the strength
searching for the faith I know
to come back and take it's place

To stay within your world
I would surely have died
this is something I must do
for I do value my own life

I fought within myself for you
but my heart you cannot win
it follows my soul where it goes
to stay would be a mortal sin

I drift back into my own realm
transcending space and time
back through the witches' door
that for you I had left behind

My spirit guides welcome me
back to the place where I belong
this is the life I know and believe
this is where I am forever strong

I look back on your world now
from the doorway to my home
I've no regrets of leaving it
for in it, I was always alone

The Temple
Written May 2001

Sanctuary of body and mind
keeper of secrets throughout all time
filled with universal power and light
guarded from all others prying eyes

Tonight there will be many
chanting and dancing will commence
the cone of power we shall build
one purpose, focused in unison

Skyclad before the goddess
drawing down the moon
we call upon the ancient ones
to help us in what we do

Guardians are there to witness
elements of power stir and grow
candles and incense are burning
as the energy continues to flow

The High Priestess sings her song
and then the spell is cast
as we release the energies
and send them to manifest

We stand within our temple
thanking the universal powers once again
for lending us their mighty forces
as our ritual comes to an end

And once the others take their leave
and the place is quiet once more
the high priestess visits the temple
gazing upon the hand painted floor

This temple is special, she built it
it holds her sweat and strength
hand painted over one month's time
as a dedication to her faith

She lays down within the circle
content, closing her azure eyes
floating within the indigo spirals
at peace, at one with the night

Retreating
Written June 2003

Drifting in a time I don't recognize, wandering in a field of dreams
floating out with open arms to a place only I seem to see

I thought life could be different and came out of my shell
I felt the love I've never known and watch it fall to hell

I wallowed in the waste of what was once happiness
and swam the seas of heartbreak as I worked to release the past

And now I ascend to the ethers, back from whence I came
lost and lonely once again but seeking beyond the gate

Back beyond the clouds where time ceases to exist
I shall heal and be reborn within the indigo mist

My Sphere
Written 2003

Hidden within a sphere, floating into space
away from this world that loves to hate
Encased from the chaos thrown at me everyday
Seeking to escape myself and the monster I became

I shall battle the demons of the past that break me down
and move on to new dimensions beyond where I was bound
I'll drift into myself, to a place I long to be
where my spirit soars and my soul flies free

Safe inside the sphere I've created around myself
I am as I should be healing within another realm

Lady Lazarus
Written June 2003

You left me colorless, wandering against my will
trying to wake up each day and live without a pill

You sucked the life from me as sure as I see you now
standing there smiling as I wallow on the ground

I'm not sure how or when my will began to leave
but within this moment, I feel a spark of me

Beware the devil's advocate for he befriends me still
and I shall ask of his force to bring back my dying will

I will become the brilliance that lights the farthest stars
and you shall drown in the blood of my heart

Nemesis
Written June 2003

Desire has left me with an ice cold heart
it cracks slowly with the heat of my anger
threatening to melt away forever

Madness slowly seeps from anguish
embedded in my mind once open
now closed to the world of love

Acid drips from the forks of my tongue
once merely pointed and quick
stinging those that come near

Claws grow from my fingertips
pain now comes from the grip
of hands that once healed

Blood tears seep slowly from my eyes
the ones you use to love
that enchanted you each night

And you stand staring in horror
at the monster you created
when you took your love away

Rattled and Rolled
Written June 17, 2003

Shake me
Break me

Chew me up and spit me out
No matter what you do to me
I'll be okay, have no doubt

Touch me if you dare
my poison flows freely
and there is nothing you can do
that will ever change me

Tie me up
Spank me

For your pleasure make me beg
You'll be the one left lonely
lying naked on the bed

You'll wake up wanting
to create a new bond
but I took what I wanted
and baby I moved on

Need me
Love me

Too bad for you
I've nothing left to give
after the hell I've been through

I'm not the woman you want
my soul was long ago lost
best not to get too comfortable
I'll rip out your heart nice and slow

Lucidity of a Kiss
Written June 21, 2003

Do I look Dangerous to you
as you watch me glide across the floor
My eyes holding you captive
looking in and entrancing your soul

You want to feel it don't you
my lovely, silky, cold caress
but your mind is dazed and lost
you're riveted to where you stand

What is it you feel now
as I walk slowly into your arms
Is it lust, horror, intrigue or fear
or can you comprehend at all

Instinctively you know I want you
that your death shall come from my lips
I wonder if you'll fight me darling
as my kiss pierces your salty skin

Through Dismal Eyes
Written July 2003

I'm walking but I don't know where
I can't think, my mind is bare

Visions lost from my youth
No dreams, they've all been used

Emotions gone without a trace
Reality disjointed, never to be replaced

Comatose I stare but see no light
Lost in the abyss of mental strife

Lothario
Written 2003

Your feral eyes seduced me
carrying me away, enchanting my soul
I am doomed to walk between the worlds
though you have claimed me as your own

We live outcast by our societies
forever running alone in time
my transformation never complete
and yet we are the same, you and I

Bound to you by the essence of the beast
the very blood that flows in my veins
our spirits meshed for all time, damned
though on you I place no blame

Together we run wild in the mists
defying the laws that nature has made
our bond for each other undying
eternal in it's grace

Physiological Hair
Written May 25, 2005

Traveling has always been my fascination
quaint little towns, being my favorite places
historical cities with ghost stories and lore
harboring antique people, adding their allure

Walking the darkened streets of St. Augustine
Brilliant colors aligned a window in steady beams
Transfixed by their wonder, I almost didn't see
The beautiful, aged woman, staring back at me

Smiling, she invited me to enter her humble abode
alabaster and glass lined the room, above and below
from an ancient puce bottle, she poured us a drink
and laughed when she saw a strange look on my face

The embossed words on the bottle, "Physiological Hair"
made me look at the liquor, wandering what was in there
she started telling me tales of bitters, sours and remedies
that through her 100 years of life, she'd tasted and seen

She spoke of unique shaped bottles, in many colorful hues
ultimately confessing, her favorite shades were of puce
carrying the richness of wine, within browns of the earth
the red of life's blood and the purples of spiritual rebirth

Swearing the simplicity of these wonders, gave her life
and the words from that bottle, reminded her of a time
when life was tasteless and her mind seemed to waste
within a world lacking depth, until they made her awake

The Dance
Written November 2002

She was dancing by the firelight
smiling as bright as the sun
as the moonlight filled the clearing
I watched as she danced on

She didn't seem to notice me
as she moved and swayed
dancing so happily in a circle
on her fingers, tiny cymbals she played

I stood there admiring her
she was full of zest and life
untouched by the outside world
so free and full of light

Barefooted she ran towards me
laughter echoing through the air
she softly grasped my hand
into her mystical eyes I stared

She pulled me towards the circle
silently to her music we danced
I found myself smiling and laughing
like a school girl filled with romance

We danced together on and on
and a strange familiarity grew
I felt as if I should know her
but I really didn't have a clue

She stopped and stared right through me
and in that moment I knew the truth
Just as I heard her softly whisper
"I've always been inside of you"

The Witch's Heart
Written November 2003

Cold as ice is what they say, the witch's heart impure
consorting with her demons and spreading chaos in the world

They say the witch's heart is full of evil things
in fact they say she has no heart because the devil took it away

If only they knew the truth and weren't blinded by ignorance
they'd learn to love the witch if only they'd want to understand

The witch's heart is pure and big as the universal light
she feels much more deeply due to her second sight

She knows what you're not saying and feels your joys and pains
trying to keep them separate and not confuse her own feelings

The witch's heart is open expanding with compassion and love
it does not turn away a kindness and forgives what most do not

She may seem cold at times but it's not for lack of love
should she open the gate too often other's emotions come in floods

The witch's heart is special for it loves unconditionally
but sometimes the witch grows tired from fighting the world's negativities

The witch's heart speaks volumes if you only care to be near
it sings softly to you now hoping that you will hear

She doesn't believe in devils nor conjure evil things
but you will find her laughing and dancing in the moonlights rays

233

The Fairy Queen
Written 1999

Deep within the forest amongst the evergreens
lives a land of fairies and their fairy queen
She watches with her steely glance for all that enters there
protecting all her children, it's best that you beware

She'll welcome you but once but heed her warning well
harm her children or her land and you'll not live to tell
The fairies are a peaceful bunch but cowards they are not
to intrude upon their solitude will surely make them hot

Mystical creatures of this world, most people do not see
but they are there my friend, behind that lovely tree
Sing with them and dance laugh at their merry ways
A fairy has a job to do to keep earth from decay

Venture in the forest but always go in peace
you never know who's watching from beneath the evergreens

The Tiny Fairy
Written June, 2003

Little whispers come to me, songs floating on the wind
I strain to hear the song but then it's gone again
I laid upon the grass and listened patiently
then I saw her there as pretty as can be

"I'll dance for you" she said "if you only set me free
I'm trapped down here, the grass is wet you see"
"My wings are wet and soggy I cannot seem to fly
but if you pick me up I'm sure that they will dry"

I gently picked her up like a tiny china doll
and placed her on a petal where I knew she wouldn't fall
And as the sun did shine her wings began to spread
like little tiny fire flies sparkling around her head

The sadness in her face began to melt away
and the tiny little fairy began dancing full of grace
When she was done she left me with a gift I can't replace
tears streamed from my eyes and there was a smile on my face

Serpent of Reality
Written June 2003

I love me, I'm so brazen
as I slither into the recesses of your mind
Riding the waves of your thoughts
twisting, delving deeper all the time

It's your deepest darkest secrets
that I come here to breathe
and I enjoy every pain I cause you
as your soul rips and bleeds

I hear your voice echoing in your mind
screaming as your adrenaline goes higher
While I play on your insecurities and fears
and seethe with sadistic desire

I am the evil secret you hide
The name you never want to speak
An eternity I've lingered here
You can't make me go, you're too weak

I know all of your tricks before you even try
and your pathetic little cries and whims
You try so hard to fight against me
I won't be defied, the battle never ends

I know you're afraid, I feel it
My passion rises with your fear
You want to stop me don't you
Try it, take a deep look in the mirror

Ah, I love the horror of it all
as your realization comes into view
All this time you searched for me
and really, I am just a part of you

Mistress of Sensuality
Written June 2003

Do you shun me? I who you once adored
Now cast aside by you for sexuality explored
Did you not hold me dear to your heart
As you took my innocence, making my soul dark

I was shamed by you in your pristine light
for it was you that promised I would be your wife
Let down by love I sought to survive
exploring within, myself I did find

Feast your eyes upon me for I am no longer ashamed
I am the essence of woman and will never be tamed
You seek absolution for the sins you've made
I seek only to be free and live life not in vain

I am now the mistress reigning true sensuality
and sadly your are nothing once denied angels wings

Butterfly of Life
June 26, 2003

Kaleidoscope wings capture me luring me away from the mundane
unto the charms of wind's fancy as you glide towards grassy planes

I'm carried away by your strength in awe of your ability for change
your wings span the centuries, freedom follows in your wake

Your colors alter within a moment adapting to the changes of time
the knowledge of the universe held safely within your eyes

Duality in perfect balance as the chaos of the world goes by
uninhibited by the terror of the ever changing tides

Within your folds you hold the most precious gift of all
the wisdom of the universe and the light that fills the stars

Souls Rejoin
Written 2003

We are to each other, what most never have
and those that do, rarely get to keep
we are the perfect balance of light and dark
dwelling in a place, where words we do not need

We are alike in so many ways, yet different
the differences being enough to make us each unique
adding a taste of challenge to our lives
yet blending us together perfectly

Our souls have been bonded for eternity
each life finding each other, no matter what we may be
born knowing that we shall find the other
aware of our bond the very instant our eyes meet

I knew as I ventured through this unknown terrain
that I would find what it was my soul did seek
when out of the shadows you steadily walked
a howl, a cry, tears of joy, our souls complete

Our adventure is merely beginning again
a new place, a new time, a new world
obstacles may come to stand in our way
but our love, like the sands of time, shall endure

Toxic Coma
Written July 2004

Poison apples on a hot summer's day
Savoring the juice in a purple haze
Screams leak from the room downstairs
But I'm half dead so what do I care

Falling deeper into the abyss
Waiting for you dear and one last kiss
I bite your tongue, as you pull away
The kiss of death I've never forgave

Reawakening
Written July 2003

Serenity has blessed my soul
the Goddess smiles upon me
wrapping me within her healing wings
Soothing me in a blanket of love and peace

Practices once given up for you
have laid waiting patiently for me
I claim the power once bestowed
unlocking it from dormancy

The energies come to witness
the quickening of my spiritual rebirth
and welcome me with open arms
as I once again walk between the worlds

Stagnant Ice
Written 2003

Winds howl, lucid dreams
Swirls of nothing, Chilling screams
Bitten in the ass by society
Stomping lives just to be seen

Heart frozen, soul on fire
Dead beat, love for hire
Lost dreams, reality gone
Pity party just for one

Etheric Battles
Written July 2003

Cosmic colors swirl around me
As the energy of the universe
Flows freely through my being

Enlightenment, I have chosen
And it has accepted me
As a warrior for it's cause

Armed for battle I stand
Within the astral planes
Awaiting the cosmic shift

Knowing many will suffer
Perhaps lose their minds
Unprepared for war

Forces foreseen in centuries past
Come once again to ruin
Fulfilling the prophecy of fate

Battles have already been fought
Some won, some lost, all important
To the salvation of ourselves

The knowledge is there
The choice is yours
The time is now

Misguided Fears
Written July 8, 2003

Excuse me but...

Why do you hate me or is it just fear
Why do you walk away whenever I am near

What makes you cling to your children as they come my way
and call out to your men that they'd better behave

Am I not friendly, courteous and kind
Why then, do you walk away from me all the time

Is it the etheric light that shines in my eyes
Do you fear I have a demon hidden inside

Is it my confidence you mistake for arrogance
or the way I sit in the grass as I softly chant

Is it the power you sense but can not explain
or the pentacle I wear around my neck on a chain

Do you really believe to the devil my soul belongs
Have you even stopped to think that maybe...

You're wrong

Shattered Glass
July 10, 2003

Tears are streaming down my face, I'm not sure if I'm breathing
I think my heart is bleeding and coming out my belly button
I wanted to tell you so many things but all I could do was say your name
and stare blankly at the page that shattered all of my dreams

There is something I need to know but I can't remember what
I think I'm suppose to work today but I couldn't raise my head up
Where are you and why did you go, none of this makes any sense
wasn't it just yesterday we made love and spent the day with friends

Maybe that was last month, oh Gods, I really just don't know
I thought you really loved me but I guess you really don't
I wish I had something to drink, I wish I had someone to hug
but most of all I really wish that someone would wake me up

Note to Self
July 10, 2003

You have wasted enough of your life on illusion
waiting for the cultivation of what once was
longing to be held by a love that is true
It's better to be alone, than to be used

You deserve to be loved in return
without manipulation, unconditionally
not starved for affection or a kind word
lied to and cheated on repeatedly

It's ok to be angry, feel it and let it go
but it's not worth clinging too
you are beautiful in ways he can't see
therefore, he is unworthy of you

Seek yourself through the rubble
of the wreckage of your heart
and love yourself all over again
today is the day your new life starts

Do Not Throw This Note Away

Dancing with Hemlock
Written July 2003

I've known many men like you
You all want the same thing
A woman with money to keep you
While you run around and play

I can plainly see you want me
As your eyes feast on my curves
You just haven't figured me out yet
As you sit carefully pondering your words

You know I'm single and rich
Since you've been asking around
But what you don't know is I know you
And your little game of cat and mouse

Unfortunate for you I'm jaded
I intend to keep all that I have
If you amuse me, I'll roll you
But it depends on the mood I'm in

I see you're ready to approach me
And begin our masquerade
Choose wisely, for if you bore me
You will wish you'd never came

You think you've got it all planned out
A helpless widow in your grasp
You've underestimated your prey
I've no problem putting hemlock in your glass

Ah, you think you're ready for me
The smiling gentleman, kissing my hand
A prelude to the perfect seduction
Let's see what fate has in store for you

Let the dance begin

Specimen
Written July 15, 2003

I hear a voice
as it screams and cries
though my lips can't move
I know that it's mine

I'm fighting myself
against being seen
but my mask won't falter
I fear society

I'm bound in chains
by rules, not mine
a picture perfect face
that smiles and lies

Trapped in a box
locked away with my heart
afraid that someone
might rip me apart

Standing in a mannequin crowd
wearing designer clothes
wishing for old jeans
and someone to hold

The money is great
benefits are divine
but I'll tell you the truth
I'm miserable all of the time

Ashes
Written July 19, 2003
Pits of pain adorn my face from the ember of your cigarette
Bruises taint my body, your hands imprinted on my neck
Razor lines cross my chest where my heart use to be
Permanent reminders of our love and how it was never meant to be

Nasci Draco Sanguis
Written July 2003

I've always known I'm not completely human
I glimpse him in the mirror sometimes
Inside me beats the heart of a dragon
black winged, golden splendor
with the earth and sky in his eyes

I can feel him inside of me thinking
as he watches the world through my eyes
feeling cramped and smothered
in a body too small for his frame
to soft for his essence and strength

He teaches me of great mysteries
of witches and their ancient ways
he explains why the earth cries
and why it's so important that we fight
to preserve it from society today

I feel his fire inside me each night
as I relax he stretches his wings
I know he is preparing to fly
as his brothers call him to battle
among the astral planes

Some how I know that I travel with him
the winds caressing my limbs
as his wings glide us through the night
on journey I seldom remember
when I wake up each day

But I know that I am wiser with each trip
stronger with each tick of the clock
more sure of my purpose in life
I'm not sure if I am a part of him
or he a part of me
but I do know...

We are one in this life

Cool
Written July 19, 2003

You can toy with my feelings
And play with my head
Making me dazed and confused
I understand your pain

So I'm cool

You can pretend nothing matters
That you've no future to look to
And close yourself off to me
Go ahead and hide

I'm cool

You can rip my heart to shreds
In one of your manic moods
And toss me to the curb
I will slowly heal

So I'm cool

Doesn't matter if you want me back
Doesn't matter if you don't
I no longer care
Your love left me numb

And that...Is cool

Native Woman
July 20, 2003

There you are hiding so far away from me
lost within this world, drowning in misery
Hidden in a darkness brought on by your pain
in the ice of a heart that hurt you in vain

People come and go with no regard to you
like you were but a puddle for them to walk through
They don't see your heart your inner beauty or grace
lost in a day and age that looks too much at race

They only see your shell, what you wear outside
they've no depth to see the love that you hide
Let the world see the dirt and decay
I see the rose that was before it melted away

I see the beauty that shines from within
not just the beautiful bronze in the color of your skin
I see the native behind your sweet smile
with the warmest heart eyes, pools from the Nile

The shine to your hair and strength of your will
the healing in your hands that hold power still
Don't let them destroy you for you are stronger than most
It's why they treat you this way, they fear what they don't know

Be calm beautiful one let your heart open once more
just shield it from the ones that you no longer adore
Let the world shun you, why should you care
laugh at their arrogance and their pity beware

Let your pain leave now, look within, you shall see
your strength is there, yourself, is all you have to be

Perfect Love and Loss
Written July 27, 20003

I saw him first at the bistro down town
across a smoke filled room his smile was devastating ,
his eyes enchanting, consuming the beauty of the room

He eyed me like candy waiting to be tasted as
he motioned for me to sit down, taking my hand in his,
raising them gently to his lips

He was the perfect suitor, charming in every way
stealing my heart in an instant as we talked softly to each other
over a bottle of red wine

We spent years together, loving each other
living in a fantasy of passion
no secrets between us or so I thought at the time

He opened the quadrant of my soul filling it with a light long lost
as he stole my heart away, holding it for ransom
and I didn't mind at all

Over night it turned to pestilence
sex games became pain, love turned to hate
equality to submission, a life of destruction and heartbreak

I was impugn to him now, living in a cage of deceit
a world of fear and anxiety
searching to end my life, to break free

I awoke one day to a gun shot, praying the bullet hit me
but it was my love, my tormentor
lying on the floor in a pool of his own blood

I wept that day for our love and how it use to be
before the insanity claimed him
and I lost my self in the nightmare of our lives

But as I sit here now at our table in the same bistro
I feel only the love we shared
as I drink a toast to him from a bottle of red wine

Because of his love and insanity
I truly appreciate being alive

Inferno
July 29, 2003

I'm burning in the rays of destruction
my scorched heart reaching out
to the fires that would consume me
begging it to take me now

In the unknown valleys of my mind
I dwell on a promise once made
stardust and wanderlust of that memory
is literally all that remains

Once unleashed by desire
and a yearning in my heart
now completely bound
by the melting popsicle of my soul

I sigh as the flames ignite me
and scatter my ashes to the winds
better to perish in the fires of hell
that to live my life completely frozen

Waste
December 2, 2003

Hearing nothing on poisoned wind
but questions unanswered for lives ripped to shreds

Harmony long gone for religious rights
spun out of proportion for God's mighty fight

Stones cast by serving hands
acid dripping off tongues of man

Sabers of denial waged to war
I watched it all and ask what the hell it's all for

Soul Seduction
Written July 2002

You called to me and I came
though you never spoke a word
I've waited in death's mist for you
watching in silence beneath my hood

I rode the fatal winds to be at your side
breathing your scent of decay
your time has come my friend
to join me in another place

Your fear of me hurts my feelings
I'm here to be your friend and guide
death has come to claim you now
and I shall take you to the other side

Would you wallow between the worlds
forever lost and crying
there is no escape from the reaper dear
please stop trying to defy me

That's it, come into my embrace
ah yes, what a couple we shall be
traveling the infinite road of death
chained together eternally

Cold Fire
Written August 2003

My glance can rivet you to the spot you stand
or beckon you closer into my embrace.
Easily tempting you with my subtle lips
as you lean gently gazing at my face.

A touch of my hand can warm your heart
or send you wishing for an early demise.
I am the brilliance you cannot fathom
The perfect balance of fire and ice

Hindsight
Written 12, 2003

Tears on my pillow is all that remains of a love
once bonded from pleasure, now pain
Seeping into the pores of my silken skin
drenching my heart with the waste of our sins

Trying to remain sane as we run away
knowing alone we can go no place
Clovers have wilted, luck has run dry
but without each other life is a lie

Coming Home (A Spiritual Journey)
Written October 2, 2003

Water washed over my body moving it out to sea
as the salts of the earth caressed and cleansed me

I drifted upon the mighty waves trying to catch my breath
no longer wishing to escape the world, just the misery I have left

I let the current carry me ever steadily towards the shore
crashing against sand and rocks, through endless nights of tears I forged

I stood as I heard her calling me upon the raging winds
singing the song of mysteries, letting me know that she forgives

The Great Mother whispered to me beckoning me to join the dance
enchanting me back to her realm to give my life another chance

And there upon the shore of the sea, a sacred circle I did cast
bringing back the powers I forgot and coming home at last

Storm of the Full Moon
Written August 6, 2003

I can sense it in the air as it drifts near to me
the power of the elements seething to be released

The earth faintly trembling as far off thunder booms
I smile softly to myself knowing it will reach me soon

Energies surge within me I can barely keep contained
as I walk to the covered deck waiting silently for the rain

Clouds of blues and grays move steadily in the sky
billowing across the moon upon it's sacred night

The winds start howling my tiny chimes sing along
as the thunder claps again the rain comes pouring down

Lightning streaks the sky so fiercely with it's light
snapping against the ground with all it's power and might

The waves are churning in a sea as gray as the sky
mist spraying up to drench me as I watch them pass by

Palm trees bend, yielding their fronds whipping in the wind
I stand in awe at the storm and it's power of destruction

I chant softly out loud knowing I shall be safe
from the fatalities of the storm and it's winds gust of rage

Somehow comforted by the beauty of it all
thankful to be a witness of Mother Nature's call

As the storm starts to calm and the waves of the sea subside
the full moon once again shining brightly in the sky

I stand at the deck's railing smiling and watching the sea
knowing that somehow part of it lives inside of me

Watch Over Me
Written August 17, 2003

Watch over me, I don't think I'm sane
wandering in the shadows, no hope and no name
Barely breathing the hot stale air
of shattered dreams, drowning in despair

I remember the light, how it used to shine
But I've lost my way, it's dark and I'm blind

Don't let me fall into eternity's sleep
I'm trying to save me, please watch over me

The Voices
Written August 16, 2001

The dead speak and so do the living
words unspoken, knowledge, thoughts in their heads
Energies that move in space waiting to be heard
comfortable in the knowledge no one else knows what's said

But there are those that do hear the chatter in the wind
the words formed in the mind just seem to come to them
Some call it a blessing, some a curse, gift or myth
but really it is something we are all born with

Perhaps you don't use it, maybe you forgot
or your religion tells you it's evil, but really it's not
Some develop their skills, they not only hear, but see
all the different forms of life, other worlds and entities

Would you open the door to the knowledge that waits
or stand behind the walls of our earthy plane?
But know it's not always pretty to know what people don't say
when you open your mind, your world will never be the same

253

Huh?

Written August 21, 2003

You look and stare
never meeting my gaze
inching closer as you speak
yet part of you backs away

I silently wait for you
to ask me what you will
but somehow you never do
but I can sense how you feel

Somehow I intrigue you
but I don't really understand
why it is that part of you fears me
I'm just a mere woman

There's nothing very special
or amazing about me
No rare beauty, I rarely smile
most the time I'm never seen

I reach out to touch your hand
I can see that you're upset
but when my fingers reach you
you pull back your hand

I turn to leave you standing
alone beneath the tree
and suddenly you whisper
"What's it like to be a mystery"

Swift as the wind you bolted
leaving me there in a daze
wondering what you meant
and why you ran away

This memory of you lingers
although you can't be found
I'd like to tell you the answer
but I've never figured it out

Deceiver
Written September 2003

There are lies and there is truth
and then...

Feelings contained left to assumptions
a tease of existence to unknown prey

Insecurities hidden in indecision
left dangling to cling, yet push away

Promises broken, Excuses made
of depression, poverty and strife

Egotistical, manic depressive
wallowing in misery, defying life

Indifference, a mask staring
in the eyes of those once used

Misconceptions of questions
left unanswered, clearly mental abuse

There are those truths hidden
which are worse than lies

Casualty of Silence
Written 2003

Self confident and poised
a tower of strength un-denied
logic and reason up front
tears hardly ever cried

The teacher, the healer
always smiling, always there
the positive thinker, the rock
in the mist of despair

Now searches for someone
to take the pain from inside
for a hug or a shoulder to lean on
tears streaming from blood shot eyes

Defeated, lonely and broken
a curled up ball on the floor
wracking sobs and whimpers
as the phone rings for her

No point in answering
they won't listen to her cries
though she tried to ask for help
they still, only wanted advice

They'll wonder what happened
once it's too late
she only needed a friend
but silence sealed her fate

Azure Fires
Written 2003

Azure fires beckon
Taunting, teasing, opening your soul

Reaching to caress you
Burning, soothing, taking control

Traveling your body
Sensually probing from the start

As you stand there
wanting , trusting, waiting for them
to claim your heart

Final Peace
Written September 10, 2003

Consumed within the depths of night
upon you wake or sleep
satin shadows caress your soul
where your heart used to be
moving over the loss and pain
numbing even your every tear
what once was feared, now comfort
to the cries that no one ever hears

And though the faint light flickers
beyond your weary grasp
beckoning with signs of hope
you pray this dawn to be your last
for all is lost in sorrows dream
reality no longer in favor
you cackle as your mind snaps
death's release the final savior

Preparing to Rise
Written November 2003

The storms I've weathered
have made me weak
though they threaten to consume
I'm still standing on two feet

I've watched the towers blow
in a blinding rage
seen the skin fall from my bones
and my blood wash away

The cutting of my heart
threatened to destroy my soul
ice melting at a glance
gates that left a gaping hole

I've retrieved the eyes
lost from my weary mind
to gaze upon the shadows
that imprisoned many times

They say the blackness
shall fill me completely one day
but I believe in a strength
that shall keep it at bay

So I stand upon the threshold
waiting once again for spring
to revive what has died inside me
and repair my broken wings

And as I watch the horizon
for a fleeting glance of you
I shall heal as you suffer
the hell you put me through

Knowing I shall live
and fly once again free
for I will never become
what you wanted me to be

Love's Rebirth
Written 2003

You sent me spiraling
into a world I thought I lost
calling me back into it's essence
to a time I had forgot

Showing me there's still life
a chance to love and shine
within a soul that's pure
and a heart as red as wine

Wrapping me in a blanket
of security and warmth
sincerity, love and passion
that I never dreamed of

I wait for you now
weaving a spell of fancy
waiting for your hand
to join me in life's dances

Your friendship brought me back
from the tunnel I was in
and for that I thank you forever
for with you, new life begins

Hollow
Written November 2003

Spiraling upon tainted winds, in the shadows I did seek
retribution for the sins that came as you washed away the whole of me
and though I'd like to laugh upon your poisoned grave
I can no longer feel the satisfaction of your demise and decay
So I slither from the site of what I thought would set me free
towards the light of nothing that's left inside of me

Final Mistake
Written November 2003

Wicked rain drops burn my skin
like cascades of liquid fire
ruining the pleasure you tainted
with your poisoned tongue of lies

From holes to burrows down my spine
the toxic acid burns it's way
to the soul I've buried from you
attempting to ignite it's gaseous flames

Speed through me with your window
of opportunities long since gone
edging your way into my life once more
when all hope, long ago was lost

I wait for you with sickle in hand
to free you from your self wrought hell
the ice maiden you've created from pain
smiling inside, knowing that I shall be

Your final mistake

Mirror Talk
Written 2003

She's there, I know
hidden deep within my being
waiting for me to step aside
with steel eyes that watch
like a predator biding her time

They say she's reckless
promiscuous with a fancy for the drink
ruthless in keeping what is hers
selfish in her actions
cunning in the way she thinks

She knows things, secrets
that you keep to yourself
using them all against you
as she plays you like a violin
into your own private hell

I fight her with all I am
tossing her aside when I awake
as I seek to find her hiding place
threatening to take all her fun
and label her insane

She comes mostly when I'm weak
hurt or wallowing in heartbreak
as I crave the touch of love
she strokes the bitterness inside
while thriving on my pain

Step away from me now
danger is within your proximity
lurking inside me, she waits
patiently for your fear
to add to her quickening

Would you linger
taunting her tortured soul
cleverly trying to delve in her mind
demons await there
and she has control

The Queen of my mind

Beyond the Mask
Written November 23, 2003

I am who you want me to be, moving in circles
waiting for you to tell me all the things that you need

My face is brilliance, a mask of deceit
beauty to behold but pain underneath

Hiding behind eyes that never seem to smile
as least they haven't in a very long while

My wit is charming, my tongue cutting edge
I could heal or destroy you, it's your choice in the end

My mind is a maze, only few get inside
to see the light in my shadows you must broaden your mind

You smile and praise my beauty and grace
but have you ever really seen beyond my face

I'm Weeping
Written November 23, 2003

I weep for the children who's parent don't care
too stuck in a world full of flash and flair

While bleeding souls cross the street
or are lying in gutters with nothing to eat

Famished for affection, covered in fleas
tarnished by a society who view them as weak

I weep for the world, for the forgotten grace
the blunder of what's left of this human race

Ruining the earth with their careless ways
leaving nothing left but death and decay

Sentiments and values shot down the drain
by jaded people and their selfish ways

I weep for the future and I pray for world peace
but you don't see my tears, your heart doesn't bleed

Invitation to be Free
Written November 2003

Enchant me with your sadness
let me delve into your soul
with a look in my eyes
and a touch of my hand
I can make you whole

Let me enlighten you with my love
flowing steadily through your being
releasing all that keeps you bound
a true union of all that we are
the greatest spark of natural healing

Come with me on the winds
to the realm of indigo fires
a world of knowledge to be hold
where time is nothing
but a window of endless desires

Ride with me on a journey
of paths you've never known
exploring what's beyond your mind
opening it to new opportunities
releasing you from all control

Opening the doors to freedom
letting your spirit roam free
into a place of mysteries
at one with the universe
the way you should always be

Surviving the Panther
Written May 16, 2004

Beneath the heat of his powerful limbs
his musky scent violated my senses
until I could only stare into topaz eyes
trembling as his breath caressed my face
silently he walked away leaving me
admiring the beauty of his onyx coat

Phantasm
Written November 24, 2003

I'm not the same as I was, time has never stood still
never allowed me to breathe, never bent its will

The winds never stopped carrying their mournful cries
of happiness long shattered on pleasure's borrowed sighs

It seems fire consumes me, eternally licking my flesh
I watch with eyes that never close, breathing in my vile stench

My screams are all that echoes in the emptiness of space
as the terror of loneliness scratches its claws at my face

Sometimes I hear reality calling from somewhere beyond my reach
I only wish it would tell me when my mind was unleashed

Be a Rebel
Written November 26, 2001

There is that which can be seen only with the mind's eye
Those that can be heard with only your heart
and that which is written that shall never come true

Why?

Because we do not allow ourselves to believe
In the things that society has taught us not too

To This I say...

Open Your Mind

Be a Rebel

Love's Limbo
Written February 8, 2004

Loved most, Shown the least
hanging by a thread of life's realities

Sanity's escape forever just a dream
for a look in the eyes of fear's passive stream

Pull me close, let me go, no explanations in confusion's web
I want to stay and make a life but wonder if I'm better off dead

Fighting within the depths of the heart's growing pains
won't break the monotony of the life you live in vain

So I ask you once again embrace me or let me flee
my love, my soul is fading inside your misery

Wilted
Written February 26, 2004

I'm teetering on the brink of insanity's edge
Wondering why you left without a word being said
Waiting for an answer not knowing what to do
Climbing the walls of silence left within this empty room

I know I've the strength to make it on my own
But I forgot where I placed it, I'm lost and alone
Wanting to hate you but my heart won't let me
Hating myself for loving you and hoping you're happy

I wander what went wrong and why I can't understand
how or when you decided to change our life's plan
I tell myself it doesn't matter, you are already gone
But how could you leave if I did nothing wrong

I know you can hear me and feel my soul bleed
yet you're being so cruel, why are you torturing me
Weren't we friends too, couldn't you tell me the truth
I'm dying inside now from the pain caused by you

Wrath of Heart
Written April 10, 2004

Do you find that which amuses you amongst the saline of my tears
as I whimper closely against you willing myself to disappear
deep within the folds of promises intuition told me were in vain
your prize, my quivering body burst into raging flames

Tormentor of my heart, like a phoenix I will fly
though forsaken by your love, my spirit shall not be denied
For immortal is my soul that shall shadow you henceforth
you underestimated my weakness my heart's wrath is your reward

266

Ending Delusions
Written April 4, 2004

Of your own free will you submerged
into the depths of my eternal fire
quickened within it's power
confused by the everlasting light
lacking the knowledge to claim it
and the will to open your mind

Now you stand in the shadow
of a heart once open and waiting
peering into the abyss of my eyes
puzzled by the lack of warmth
as you seek to remove me from my world
into the ignorance of your life

Delusions shroud your perception of me
you've never looked beyond the veil
deep beneath my skin, into my soul
to the truth of what you see as insanity
the very essence of existence
the mysteries that the universe beholds

Our time is over, paths long chosen
dwelling in different worlds of vows unspoken
there's nothing of me that you can claim
no power you hold to bend my will
you're only a memory of what never became
a promise spoken from mundane hell

Purebred Shadows Revealed *(Acrostic)*
Written May 19, 2004

Purity caked in the blood of their youth
Under blankets of lost innocence and dreams
Rise from the debris cast upon them
Each breath a struggle for freedom unseen
Bestowing their hearts upon all of mankind
Reaching beyond a system where they are denied
Egos of the hierarchy they've never possessed
Divorced from the glamorous privileges of life

Slaves to the stations passed down from old ways
Hold fear and oppression against humanity's growth
Aristocrats stand freely and look down their noses
Dowsing all facets of faith as they strive to kill hope
Openly displaying disgust and disdain
Whispering jokes in their circles of blue collar ways
Silently wishing they could share their bed for one day

Riches can not free them from their bonds
Enchanted chains that threaten the rip out their soul
Vigorously they want the boredom to die
Envisioning a life with real friends to make them whole
At the top of society they've come to be fake
Leaving a sense of esteem that they just can't place
Equality is the answer and we all hold the key
Deserted the lock waits for self deceptions to leave

Fantasia's Sorrow
Written May, 2004

I could drown within
the sea of your sorrow
or fly within unworldly colors
swirling webs of fantasy

Dreaming of cotton candy
touching my tongue
or of your hands shaking
as your addiction touches me

Would you have me stare
into the wounds you make
or feast my sultry eyes
upon the rising sun

Shall I let the moon beams
caress my silken skin
or watch the bruises
surface one by one

Yes, I could silently drown
within the sea of your sorrow
our misery accompanying me
as our love slowly dies

But I chose to break free
and remember being happy
rather than stay with you
and pray for my demise

Quickening of Spirituality
Written May 2002

The shimmer of the moon
upon waters running deep
sun bathing the shores
winds rushing through the trees
bird songs and winter
lightning storms and rain
all stir within me energies
renewing all my faith

A child laughing
lovers holding hands
friendships that warm hearts
the embrace of a strong man
scents of flowers in bloom
springing from the earth
these are the things that call
upon my spiritual rebirth

Spirits continue to speak
showing visions to me
stones quicken my soul
as they brush against bare feet
healing heat from hands that know
stirring elemental energies
these are the wonders
that I live and breathe

Seeking what most fail to see
beyond this world of mysteries
ancient teachings, olden ways
gliding among astral planes
dragons eyes in purple haze
making me who I am today
a spiritual being of golden light
living here in human guise

River of Gold
Written June 2004

I walk alone within a river of gold
Through dark mist, lingering near
In a realm they fear to venture
Protected by the pentacle I wear

Through dark mist, lingering near
Screams seem to fall and rise
As claws rake against my aura
They disappear into the night

In a realm they fear to venture
Brilliance and wisdom wait for me
Skyclad in their embrace, I quicken
An untamed spirit roaming free

Protected by the pentacle I wear
Within my mind of indigo dreams
Silver cords bring me back to earth
Enlightened with the mysteries

Protected by the pentacle I wear
In a realm they fear to venture
Through dark mist, lingering near
I walk alone within a river of gold

Lost in the Sunset
Written May 2004

The veil of our world beckons me
to step forth and venture beyond
quivering within the serenity
of its timeless, endless power

I no longer crave to just fly
but soar into the brilliance

As the winds caress my soul
and its beauty touches my eyes
within that moment I always know
that I shall never truly be alone

Shudder
Written 2000

Within my hollow walls of warmth
you seek a stirring unsurpassed
that holds your pleasure captive
awaiting the sea of my aftermath

Sighing as you shudder against me
your essence mingling with mine
I feel my power over your gender
as you collapse between my thighs

And while you drift off to dreamland
I shudder as I breathe in your scent
stirring passions within my soul
that I vowed never to let back in

Lonely Dreamer
Written June 13, 2004

Do I haunt you, staring wide eyed
through the lace chains of your heart
as I threaten to destroy the shell
that keeps your world from falling apart

Desperate in the guise of love
carrying tentacles of your pain
Leaking stolen tear drops
from my blood shot eyes in vain

Do I haunt you, wake and sleep
behind the veil of Summerland
beckoning for you to follow me
through eternity, to hold my hand

Or am I just a vision, a fantasy
created within your mixed up mind
reaching out to take control of you
as though your heart were mine

Stolen Moments
Written June 15, 2004

Orange blossoms on the wind
the taste of sugar on my lips
the wind brushing my cheek
cool satin against my skin

This is all I need
in a world full of pain
to make me smile again
like a child waiting to play

Until the real world comes
and slaps my innocence away
leaving me with un-cried tears
on a grown up, stone face

Aftershock
Written June 27, 2004

Blindly staring in awe
into satin stained sheets
trembling in the aftermath
of twice forbidden heat

Volcanic eruptions
leaving no energy
to roll from the abyss
of alabaster dreams

Sleep eluded
by dark haunting eyes
dripping blood let tears
of impassioned cries

Iron caressing tongues
taking sorrow away
turning pain to pleasure
in a life of the mundane

Grasping at threads
of black garments adorned
with the beaded embrace
of jewels carelessly sown

Writhing in sheets
sweat pouring, juices flow
impassioned, imprisoned
tied and torturously slow

Whimpering as the salt
seeps into small wounds
tethers unleashed
fantasy gone to soon

Reaching in the darkness
seeking long graceful legs
a silhouette fills the doorway
leaving a trembling daze

Salt My Wounds
Written July 17, 2004

Salt my wounds, won't you
for it was you that put them there
searing them softly in my flesh
with hands of cruelty and despair

Your confusion is so touching
spilling from this one lone sober day
tears leaking as you crawl towards me
begging me to love you and to stay

Won't you take but a moment
to reflect upon the misery
inflicted on a heart now lost
to an illusion of our wedding rings

I've adorned your love in colors
brilliant purples, blues and greens
upon the flesh you once caressed
through years of drunken screams

I've prayed to die a thousand times
emotionally lost to friends and family
the life we created, you took away
with an addiction that is plain to see

So salt my wounds, won't you
give me one last merciful embrace
for they tell me I shall surely die
the next time that your temper breaks

Purple Hues
Written June 10, 2004

As one lone drop of dew
slid down the window pane
I wondered in silence
if I should take your name

Smiling radiantly to myself
imagining the color of my gown
I gazed into my reflection
on the glass as the sun went down

Touching the purple hues
that stared boldly back at me
feeling the signs of your love
and how painful it could be

On that day cleansed in rain
I broke free of denial's shell
taking away the foolishness
of love's invitation to hell

I've never regretted that day
or missed your love's purple hues
but sometimes when it rains I wonder
if anger's addiction ever left you

Phantom Hands
June 17, 2004

Blindly stroking they come, like whispering winds
caressing and teasing energies lying within
awakening the dormant to a heightening pitch
a fevering frenzy upon a glaciers wish

Untamed and unleashed with no rhythm or rhyme
lingering and taunting their essence divine
beckoning glimmers the eyes fail to see
as the body shudders within the mind's ecstasy

Taming the Beast
Written August 30, 2004

Beneath the moons glow, I watch
obsidian sheen caressing my eyes
displaying all I require to know
transcending beyond space and time

Shadowed mist, as cool as ice
moves me weightlessly, where I may
gaze into emerald eyes that lie
To that I am, you can not hold sway

Within an embrace that encumbers
phantoms leeching for what you stole
you beseech me, to be denied
betrayal's loss seethes beyond control

Your craving shall go un-peaked
for I am the nightmare, never refused
forged from the purity of a true love's heart
disclosed in my eyes, transfixing hues

Consequences come as promised
displayed before my heart, I gave
passion cut from a lustful groin
by a dragon freed within your game

You greatest fear released, vengeance
for battered flesh and murdered trust
a lifeless sheath between strong thighs
befitting justice for your rapist touch

Shuddering in withdrawal, I turn
drifting back from whence I came
through the doorway of obsidian
beyond the mirror, my soul forgave

Etheric Dance
Written August 2003

I need not see that which arrives
though I do through eyes of three
called within this sacred place
upon the ancient powers that be

Compass points at beck and call
guardians standing within the gates
allowing only energies I require
for what I will and the form it takes

Azure hues of mist roll round
securing paths between the worlds
in a moonlit ball, a goddess' dance
throughout the Ethers shall be heard

Limbs hold steady, a quivering frame
taking it all through head and toe
a circuit blue inflamed within
building power within the cone

Two eyes closed, the third alive
visions building, holding strong
tongues roll words of ancient ways
incense smolder, sweat pours on

Golden wings shield a duo's embrace
heightening euphoria of the soul
building painfully sweet ecstasy
power a priestess comes to know

Etheric eyes gleam possession
of the divinity proclaimed within
with the words "So Mote it Be"
enchantments release upon the wind

Spread the Light
August 2003

Shifts fill the universe with changing tides
it's a fight some will win, some shall lose
many know not what befalls them or why
but feel as though they may lose their minds

People are changing in many ways
those that are spiritual tend to understand
forces that guide, others that destroy
it's a war waged in the universe before man

Spiritual warriors battle in the ethers
forces stir here in the veils of the earth
it's our choice to stand and fight or die
to wither away or prepare for rebirth

There is and shall be confusion
issues buried coming forth to deal a hand
the scattering of thoughts and depression
it's important to let it flow, but do no give in

Light workers are sought out for their healing
not only by spiritualist, but the mundane
the subconscious mind opening their intuition
they come as though beckoned in some way

Spirituality is being questioned
beliefs are torn apart and being destroyed
wars waged against religions in vain
each blaming the other for the holy wars

The time has come for us all to unite
no matter the religion or creed
the higher power calls to us all
to spread healing and positive energies

Call it good and evil or opposing forces
light or darkness, the devil and god
Call it what you will, in what you believe
but as humanity we must unite for the good of all

The veil between the worlds grown thinner
dimensions move and intertwine
our earth, our lives are what's at stake
isn't that more important than religious fights?

May we all stand together in spirit
spreading the light upon our world
healing it and each other as one
and bring peace again for us all

279

Time's Fury
Written August 2004

Time shall have its fury
raging within nature's ways
though passed on and forgotten
through it, our earth decays

Fighting against our ignorance
as we let it slowly waste away
it screams what we've forgotten
bold and surely in our face

Tears weep from the air we breathe
settling into the essence of our soil
trying to cleanse and defy our abuse
as we thanklessly kill the rain forest

Our world continues against strife
as we carelessly ignore the signs
that the earth on which we dwell
watches us cause our own demise

Yes, time shall have its final fury
raging at us within nature's ways
for we listened not to universal pleas
that would have kept it from decay

Jest of Fate
Written April 7, 2005

You feel me, I know
my sultry eyes caressing
moving against your frame
lowered as you walk by

Years gone, I've watched
graces of a panther striding
entrancing me, taunting
as I feel your essence

Have you always known
amused by my fascination
my sudden burst of heat for you
a flare nearly out of control

No, I never fantasize
merely dare myself, reaching
upon astral trips, lust to pleasure
wondering if you'd tame me

Your eyes mirror sometimes
our lips, parting to explore
subtly stopping, meeting my gaze
body quivering, I'd meld to yours

Would you take me, quite worthy
my spirit powerful, yours knows
Or does society rule me, a conflict
A "wog", a joke, nothing more

Embracing Love's Shadow
Written June 28, 2005

They say love is everything, in every vision that we see
But it never laid its arms around a wretched whore like me

Lust cradled hidden passions, in brazen woos for men's desires
seeking only a chest to lay upon in the early morning hours

Kisses rained and seed spewed forth, clinging to moistened thighs
heated bodies, never lingered through the coolness of the night

Morning's light hit swollen eyes, like a brutal stab of pain
pulling dreams of utter bliss into reality's cruel domain

Hoping hands reached for limbs, finding only dirty sheets
remembering a passion filled night, lost to lonely sleep

As I gaze into the mirror, at the face that stole my name
I stare into the changing eyes, shadowing my heart's pain

Wondering where the woman went, that longed for love's dream
of holding hands and waking up, listening to someone else's heartbeat

But in that glass I only find, a used up wretched whore
who thought someone could love her, but will wish it... never more

Liquid Grace
Written June 29, 2005

Tempered peaks
of azure hues
streak lightning's fatal kiss
as charcoal billows
gust and twirl
waves of nature's wish

Crystalline tears
leak in unison
though each one unique
as they fall
upon the waiting earth
from darkened cotton sheens

Fresh linen scents
destroy stagnant air
lingering on heightened winds
while scorched terrains
sigh their relief
upon rising opaque mist

I stand erect
bare feet in the grass
with arms outstretched
feeling cool drops pelt me
cleansing my aura
of life's dismal effects

As silken hair blows freely
riding the storm's ebb and flow
I brazenly dance
to the tune of the rain
tasting its sweet nectar
in smooth swallows

Stillness finds me
lying naked
upon weathered plains
smiling softly to the sky
as I thank it for cleansing me
in its rays of liquid grace

Shower for Two
Written June 29, 2005

Sweat glistens
against olive skin
as amber bottles
enjoy a dewy caress

Cool shades
hide my hungry glance
while it roams to feast
upon a hairless chest

I watch him often
through summer days
his tanned essence
taunting my senses

Engines roar
their union sublime
his motor humming
with the purr of my desire

Cold beer in hand
I beckon his attention
always eager to please
my object of fascination

He stops, I stand
sunglasses fading away
as I hold him captive
within my sultry gaze

Fresh cut grass
lingers in the air
as I wipe down his legs
with my hands bare

Soon silken strokes
lead to a shower for two
lost in an embrace
of a lover's summer moon

History's Cries
Written June 30, 2005

Antiquated, they linger
memories locked in time
superior to woes and chaos
disenchanted hearts left behind

Death's cobwebs, merely dust
forgotten in stagnant air
imprisoned by careless whispers
trying to hide life's despair

Treasures of wonders, lay
beckoning senses of the mundane
as they await echoed footsteps
to unlock their secret domain

Opaque essences cry softly
resurrection their only dream
rotting slowly, denied recognition
from eyes too modern to see

Disenchanted hearts left behind
superior to woes and chaos
memories locked in time
antiquated, they linger

Tainted
Written July 2, 2005

I am tainted by the beauty of you
the poison on which I feast my eyes
my heart once golden with our love
now holds only charred ashes inside

I watch you sleeping as though in a dream
there is no escape from the vision of you
the splendor of your essence glowing
as I lay here once again feeling used

You cut me to the quick repeatedly
as your tongue becomes a dagger of lies
yet once again I've lost myself in the abyss
of your darkened passion filled eyes

Sweet surrender of the soul is all you ask
as you leisurely bide your time
locking me away like a secret
so no one knows of our passionate ties

I am tainted by the love we once did have
clinging to a shimmer of hope that would not die
I've remained here with you an animated corpse
awaiting the moment your depression subsides

Tonight my love, before you wake
I whisper to you one last good bye
leaving with only the clothes on my back
to join the phoenix and once again fly

Ariana (The Lost Faerie)
Written July 2003

She lived in the midnight forest
where life is full of peace
but ventured into our world
to find such desolate misery

Thinking she could change it
she tried with all her might
but the fairy she became
would give anyone a fright

Once beautiful and shiny
her wings of silver shone
but now she's torn and tattered
and cannot fly back home

She stood along the river bank
hoping her family would come
but they just flew right by
leaving her desperate and alone

She had her dreams and hopes
but no one else believed
and the wondrous little fairy
gave up on all her dreams

Barely living, without a care
on an earth, she now despised
never once in all these years
has she ever sat and cried

Now she walks shadowed banks
playing tricks on all that come
they never knew what hit them
Ariana had come undone

Destruction Denied
Written July 3, 2005

Fashion me a lifeline of the disdain that you harbor
through all your self righteous fathoms of the truth
brought forth from your ever growing, god-like persona
for I shall eat it up, inch by inch in a impassioned frenzy
as though I were starving for the taste of blood

While you gorge upon the hearts of those around you
and fill your mind with fanciful games of amusement
pretending not to wallow in your own misery of life
self created by the rules that are imposed upon whims
to keep yourself restrained from the reality of you

And as I devour the last piece of your spiritual essence
I shall growl with the glory and vengeance of the dragon
staring into your blue passive, vacant and dying eyes
while running my tongue across my lips, slowly smiling
knowing that you've never touched the power I hold inside

Dead is Better
Written April 9, 2006

Ancient ways, stir echoes of life in tempting ways
beneath hidden mountains where earth churns decay

As shadow's power peaks promising resurrection of life
hearts beat in anticipation of healing death's strife

Vengeful corpses triumph over sweet sacrilegious whims
wielding monstrosities of love once buried with their sins

And to the living, cries the winds warnings of crossing divinity's plan
remember, dead is always better once fate has played its hand

Crusted Saline
Written August 13, 2006

Lingering sentiments
encrust misery's fate
stealing dormant glimpses
ebony mists move to fade

Leaking silver streams
upon taupe silken flesh
a heart's hollow denial
the soul's beckoning twist

Empowered, it churns
waves of indigo spirals
self preservation, its life
the mind refreshed, smiles

Secrets test silent lips
energies, kaleidoscope dreams
spirit emerges in fantasia
renewing vows, self esteem

Fused Psyche
Written August 20, 2006

Instilled within opaque visions
formaldehyde dreams hover
in wheat fields, as if born there
destiny's tears, seek resurrection
of porcelain facades cast asunder
by mundane delusions of grandeur

White noise echoes the violation
while the assault of past lives
tortures the soul, uninterrupted
by vain cries leaking acid of mercy
burning beyond flesh to the soul
toiling affections lost, victories gone

Vapors of reality coil in reflection
spellbound in the essence of hope
a union of phantoms hiss release
congregated as one, empowered
within acceptance of their entity
the reality of spirit, they've become

Universal Light
Written July 2, 2006

Barefoot, our spirits meet
soul to soul, star to star
ablaze in the serenity
brought in kindred hearts

Embracing light, shadows
the sadness of humanity
hearing, feeling their woes
skirting fine lines of reality

Trials of life venture forth
engaging bonds, uncontrolled
as warriors beyond a realm
refusing destruction's hold

On earth, union may falter
thousands of miles span
yet, upon etheric waves
as one, we heal and chant

Omnipotent, omnipresent
guiding wills of enchantment
entwined in silver cords
the ultimate manifestation

Whispers & Moans
Written June 25, 2006

Encumbered souls
leak saline etchings

Flesh bore spores of reality
rising to the occasion
on cue of sublime cackles
released in dead eyes
and false smiles

A fabulous affirmation
of misery's denial
in the cultivation of life

Society's snide remark
of imperfections
peak the heart's demise
tantalizingly slow

Gorging pleasures
sheer whimsical facades

Butterfly light waves
dreaming hollow essences
in orgasmic proportions

Wet sheets, evidence
of loneliness to come

Ascension
Written June 25, 2006

Temperance reigns memories
churning lost dreams, reality
consequences denied in haste
forgotten lovers, chaotic scenes

Voids of opportunities seeking
fulfillment, caress the soul
mirrored in eyes of loneliness
running amuck, the mind toils

Sobs to silence, sorrows fade
as self empowerments rise
manifesting webs of pathways
coursing energies of survival

Enlightenment breathes love
of life and all that it shall hold
awakening beauty of a woman
unleashed, to rule her world

Bliss
Written February 2005

Scarves dance like kaleidoscope dreams
Withering dismal shades of gray
Alone in the aftermath of lust
As the world slowly fades away

Androgyny (Magician of Life)
Written October 31, 2005

Androgynous it fills us
empowering and sacred
universal tides of light
lurking in the higher mind

Patiently awaiting our embrace
as we fight to balance forces
of femininity and masculinity
cultivating our true being

Primal needs stir in echoes
passions, strengths and needs
striving to break the barriers
to trust intuitive instincts

Emotions teeter, walls erect
stifling the nurturing in us all
as the warrior rules the caverns
bending our will to cruelties call

Therein lies the dark abyss
the tainted passions, broken lives
black widows seeping poisons
willing tortured souls to die

Balance seeks to be obtained
within the vessels of our bodies
the feminine, gentle mother
the warrior, our brazen father

Mating with each other
twirling our senses within spirals
of sublime serenity for our taking
the perfection of self upon us

Androgynous, we accept
the true and everlasting light
maintained within the balance
of all that's sacred and divine

The perfection of us, the magician
the manifestation of our own lives

Hot Coffee on a Winter's Day
Written October 30, 2005

Two days driving by, I noticed him
the reason why, I couldn't explain
nothing about him stood out
each day, he looked the same

His clothes were beige and white
though old, they seemed clean
his coloring and features, plain
yet, clearly he needed me to see

I could tell he was disturbed
his energy didn't feel quite right
so I'd studied him as I sat patiently
at the same intersection's light

Day three, again he sat there
it was raining, he looked so cold
so I pulled over and walked to him
wondering just what I was doing

He smiled warmly as I spoke
reaching out to take my hand
then said "Can we go to breakfast?"
"I've missed you, my darling Ann"

That's when I saw the sticker
pinned sternly to the pocket of his shirt
written boldly was a number and said
"If I get lost today, please call my son."

We walked to a nearby coffee shop
and I called his son, right away
the poor old man had wondered off
and been lost for three days

As we waited for his son to arrive
I listened to tales of his youth
all the while, he called me Ann
repeating that he loved my new perfume

Ann was his wife of thirty years
his son, eagerly explained to me
as we put Edgar into the car
on his way back home to safety

Sometimes I think about him
always praying that he's safe
thankful for the voice of intuition
that made me stop on a winter's day

295

Enlightening Dance
Written August 24, 2005

Iridescent lights twinkle
like an hour glass of time
working wonders into miracles
by the busy street side

Colors splashing brilliance
religion's honor in your face
she cultivates the knowledge
of her cultures heritage

She sings and dances
inviting you into her world
smiling graciously
taking your sweaty palm

Twirling you to victory
through inhibitions lurking near
until you feel euphoria
spurring you on

And there fascination reigns
in the hollows of your mind
filling it with the richness
of a culture, once thought dying

She takes your hands
as she smiles into your soul
reinforcing words
that were never truly spoke

Shaking her head to money
when your dance is done
she places beads about your neck
with an act of sheer love

You want a picture, for memory
she's so happy to oblige
so you'll never forget her eyes
telling secrets of olden times

Wrapped in the innocence of a child
keeping her culture alive

Bleaching Life
Written on July 26, 2005

Cleanliness impresses me
sterile scents drifting, denying germs
signifying consciousness to the grime of life

This path, I've walked, compulsive
seeking perfection in the illusion of control
as I wondered aimlessly

Gaining realization that in reality it means nothing
compared to sentiments of a cozy home
with toys on the floor

Yet I clean, letting chlorine fill my lungs
until I choke watching flesh peel
from fingers too weak to hold up to its power

All for a bleach scent burning my nostrils
cluttering taste buds, ruining gourmet scents
emanating from stoves labored over in love

Only to fabricate the perfect picture
in the minds of a society that no longer views nature
as anything but filth needing cleared away

Asking myself why we seek to kill that which adapts
in seconds with only destruction in mind
while our immune systems wither away to nothing
as we bleach away life

Sanctity of Soul
Written July 8, 2005

Spiraling ritual antiquities accent billowing
~flames~
embracing mists of purification's enlightenment

Illumination the doorways key to complexity's
~simplicity~
drifting silently upon realms of prayers

Ancient wood cascades scents of sacred offerings
~un-denied~
by energies spiritual, physical, astral or mundane

Solidifying consecrated grounds of worship in
~divinity's light~
the sublime acceptance of faith undefined

Sandalwood's aroma lingers long after\ the demise of
~silence~
beckoning you to make a stand uninhibited by fears

In a lost world awaiting sanctity of soul

Dryer Violation
Written July 22, 2005

Who left the dryer on anyway?

In a sweat box, filled with nuts
standing there, vomit induced
by this foul stench, emanating
like a cross between popcorn
burnt to a crisp, in a plastic bowl
and putrid, burning flesh

Don't they see them?

Spinning like tops, banging
heavily against glass doors,
their soles sticking like glue
as they churn relentlessly,
barely displaying blue tongues,
as they break Laundromat silence

I bet they would if...

Those were their satin panties
entwined with shoe strings,
clinging to the tentacles of
rubber slobber, quite violated
by the ignorance of man,
as they screamed in pain

But then again...

Who cares if they rented a space,
paying their hard earned dollar,
taking care to destroy their own
articles of clothing with stupidity
as they left them unattended to
play video games next door

I know I don't, I'm only passing by

Traveling Purple Hues
Written June 19, 2005

Lavender scents drift
hazing my mind
encumbering me in sorrow
though I know it isn't mine

I seek it, crave it
delving into its Indigo hues
silently wallowing as I search
the soul that craves my use

Soft whispers echo,
my name hanging adrift
lulling me to a place of darkness
of where I no longer exist

Pale violet eyes, plead
yearning for rays of my light
as they transmit the pain
lost within their heart's sigh

She stands, a fallen angel
drowning in emotions of plum
willing an embrace to take away
the foul essence she's become

Cradling in her arms, I wept
the tears she'd never cried
restoring the fallen angel
with the purple pizzazz of life

Dismissal
Written March 2005

Spirit to spirit we touch, flesh escaping our paths
so doubt fills the mundane and passion shall never last
On this rainy night you shall come greeted by a guardian at my gate
and there you'll know the truth, your power over me holds no sway

Peeking Beyond
Written June 19, 2005

Steady streams of energies flow
captivating my senses
in a whirlwind fascination
traveling spiritual rainbows

Reaching my peak, it lingers
right there, in the mind's eye
taunting in waves of indigo
spiraling like spiny fingers

Divine light seeks my attention
willing me above and beyond
into golden splendor
leading to the white light of eternity

Floating within indigo and gold
cleansed by haunting silhouettes
past life visions peak
churning emotions
at breakneck, restless speed

A tower of light, I become
powerfully glowing, quite serene
bathed in waves of euphoria
as the spirit breathes inside me

Sacred Union of Beltane
Written June 17, 2005

The veil thins between the worlds,
as the Seven Sisters, we await
witnessing as they ride the crest
of Pleiades cosmic wave

Bel-Fires light the waning dark
beckoning the Sun God, to awake
as he peaks the eastern horizon
carrying with him, Summer's reign

Chants honor his outstretched arms,
invoking blessings and protection
as we dance and sing, intoning
to the tune of his resurrection

Between Bel-Fires, we steadily pass
making sure to encircle thrice
ensuring good luck and prosperity
through the season's birthing rite

Celebrations continue adorned,
in flowered hues and bountiful feast
as the wheel turns on in splendor
consummation of fertility peaks

Energies rise and fuel the soils
the Goddess lost in the God's embrace
upon this day of days, they mingle
reviving life, as we celebrate Beltane

Enchantment of the Muse
Written June 13, 2005

Tears fall
glimmering
from burnished eyes
of an ancient muse
recycling creativity
upon earth's bed
renewed

Molten elegance
woven
streaming fiery reds
and rust-like hues
swirling haphazardly
into liquid gold
melding, timeless
infused

Cool waters
caress
tears of copper sheen
tempering chaos
as it renews the essence
of once shattered
dreams

Nature silently
beckons
awakening passions
of a sleeping muse
sunlight fueling thoughts
to manifestation
when she is called upon
by you

Livin' Sassy
Written June 10, 2005

They never could tame me
with their earth toned hues
stiff and dowdy, like robots
carrying sophisticated blues

Stone faces, like zombies
merely walking through life
their blinders never allowing
passions to wake up and thrive

I've always danced to my own tune
brilliant, vibrant hues of pinks
purple essences opening worlds
as I seek the knowledge I crave

Fiery phantasm still moves me
beyond the world of the mundane
past the humdrum captivity
that society's rules dictate

Roaming wild and free, I blossom
upon petals of orchid enchantment
revealing reds and golds of the sun
and the moon's white glowing essence

No, they shall never tame me
for my soul belongs to fantasies
carried upon the winds of nature
alluring me to delve in their mystery

Memories of Coral Mischief
Written June 6, 2005

She sent me spinning
back to younger days
into a tie-dyed purple haze
singing along with Billy Joel
by the river near her home

No cares in the world
at least that showed
dancing along the grassy shore
scarves of pink and peach
blending like coral mischief

A broad white hat
flung purposefully in the air
brought laughter to the crowd
and no one could resist her
when she paused to pout

Men stared in awe
admiring her simple beauty
her head never turning their way
laughing, she'd just face the sun
lost to the heat of the day

Running to my side
sultry eyes and coral cheeks,
paused to grace me with her smile
as I saw myself dancing, years ago
possessing her free spirited style

Illusion of Royalty (Emerald Green)
Written June 5, 2005

There's something so...

Regal

Hauntingly noble in tone,
as it charms its way in.

With the stability of fertile earth reigning,
like a megalith emanating power,
covered in vibrant green mosses.

It holds you steadily

Within a mist of enchantment,
as it beckons you closer.

Lingering almost like an embrace,
as it envelopes you in confidence,
like a shroud of springtime's hills.

It glares, intensely

Prosperity stemming from its richness,
as it wills you to seek abundance.

An unobtrusive sense of well being,
rolling over you like aloe gel,
tempering the heat of the flesh.

Phantasm reaches, enticingly

Captivating you like fresh green herbs,
assaulting your senses in waves.

Until your mind just screams,
to delve into emerald surroundings,
lost in the illusion of royalty.

Old Swing, Margaritas and the Sunset
Written May 11, 2002

Phantom waves of heat bounce from the streets
as I lounge upon the rickety porch swing thinking
Tail lights in the distance of the one who just left
He's gone off to start anew with a woman out west

that boy is in love, he always has been
with a woman twice his age with fourteen kids
he follows her now, leaving us here alone
but what can I do, it's his life, he's full grown

So I just lean my head back and listen to the sounds
adjacent from the very water where I once almost drown
knowing once more I will swim it's strong current
if it wants to take me down, it's it right I'm intruding

lovers on the shore romping hand in hand
children screaming and playing in the sand
I wait for the one that sets my heart aflame
to come back from the boat with fish in hand

this porch swing and I, we go way back
it knows all my secrets, the good and the bad
I lost my virginity right here on this swing
spent countless nights crying here over many things

this swing loves tequila, it always has
there is not a time I've not spilled it on it's behalf
but it waits for me to stretch out and relax
cradling me every night as I watch the moon dance

sweat covers me, making my hair wet
as I sip a margarita and lick salt from my lips
taking the ice from the glass, I see him appear
I run it down my neck slowly, between my breast it disappears

all the while my fisherman, holds my sultry glance
as he walks up the porch, fresh fish in hand
leaning down he licks the water from my chest
and whispers, come on baby let's go get wet

he pulls me up gently into his arms
carrying me to the sea that he once saved me from
he believes the ocean sent me to him
and I believe with him my life finally began

307

Petals Of Destiny
Written June 2, 2005

Spring breezes taunted
like memories of a lover's hand
draping my body in caresses
as I walked slowly in silence

Pausing to close my eyes
deeply breathing in nature's scents
visions clouded my euphoria
filling my senses, of only him

Emotions churning in waves
encased my heart within their grip
seeking absolution for denying love
by never revealing its secret hymn

Upon rays of the dying sun
I raised my head in solemn vow
that should I find a rose this day
its color's message I would carry out

Entering an overgrown garden
a bleeding heart searching for hope
destiny dealt its hand upon the mystery
of the eggplant petals of the Black Rose

Lost within deep purple hues
one lone tear streaming down my face
I realized that death had met the dream
of sharing life within my love's embrace

Her Friendship
Written August 2004

Her friendship comes in hues of a rainbow's beam
embracing us tenderly like an angel's wings
with the humor of a jester and the heart of a queen

Love flows through her like a never ending stream
untainted or jaded by the world's hurtful things
Her friendship comes in hues of a rainbow's beam

When tears fill our eyes she's there on the scene
to lend a shoulder of comfort and a soul that sings
with the humor of a jester and the heart of a queen

Always sharing our hopes and cheering as we dream
like a breath of fresh air on the first day of spring
Her friendship comes in hues of a rainbow's beam

There's something about her that keeps us serene
as she guides us through all the currents life brings
with the humor of a jester and the heart of a queen

She shall always be held in the highest esteem
wrapped within our love and it's protective rings
Her friendship comes in hues of a rainbow's beam
with the humor of a jester and the heart of a queen

Hollow Depths
Written March 2005

Golden rays cloud the jade
for it lies with its intent
seeking only to break a heart
that lay dormant and content

Though it's pain brings laughter
in lusts reign of the sublime
the forked tongue of imperfection
leaves doubt within a weary mind

Sandstone Mermaid
Written May 26, 2005

Serenity taunted her from waters of aquamarine
promising warm embraces of the sun and earth
carrying her forward upon cool glimmering waves
to land clumsily, against the sands of her rebirth

Knowing her stay would be brief, upon solid land
she partook of the scents and rich green plants
letting their beauty fill deep, hollow places inside
where her vibrant heart's luster, had slowly died

As Neptune appeared, calling her back to the sea
finally at peace, she defied him, refusing to leave
enraged the God stirred the seas, calling the winds
burying her within the soil, she'd chose to stay in

Sitting silent, remembering the colors of serenity
unafraid as her stiff body fused to her beloved land
as the last grains of mist, slowly covered her eyes
she smiled immortalized, within warm silken sands

Short Circuit
Written July 7, 2005

Cold steel
clambering trays glistening in pristine lights
defying warmth of healing hands with reality's edge
of weakness showing in broken bodies

White marble glaring intensely
as it dares feet to touch
slick Lysol coated remembrances
of death clinging stagnant to life

Defenseless, I stand perplexed in sterile winds
Reeking of alcohol, staining rubber gloves
with illusions of protection
As they come, non-stop...

Visions...

Twirling me in bloody cries
smiling wrinkled faces, newborn babes
cancer ridden children seeking colorful release of bravery
lost in life's dissension

Voices...

Calling between realms
accompanying starving hands
wielding cries that reach dragging my aura to the ground
survival their instinct and so is mine

Empathy...

Running amuck
their pain, my pain, their joy, my joy
their death, my death
encumbering me until I run, crying in confusion

Escaping through doors of glass
beyond emergency rooms and hospital gates
breathing deeply of the stale air of life
alone

Prelude to Vengeance
Written February 2005

Once pleasure is lost in pain
The games come to an end
For in the temptation for salvation
Destruction is what shall win

Gates of Summerland
Written June 27, 2005

Tempest winds, stir desert heat
billowing against the western sky
upon crests of lightning's waves
spirits call, as they steadily rise

Their sorrow lifts in dusty swirls
carried away from scattered bones
as their souls gently meld together
freed from their desolate homes

Starling Owl and Yellow Moon
seek each others warm embrace
as buffalo roam with howling wolves
mingled in clouds of tangerine haze

Together they ride a majestic steed
waving good bye to ancestral lands
their journey ending in blazing light
at the gilded gates of Summerland

Hawaiian Tropic
Written June 25, 2005

As I watch the rolling waves
I can smell it
mingled in tainted pristine sands
against bronze flesh
Lurking there
as sweat tries to violate
the sanctity of its glistening union

I've never understood
the sensual essence of it
transfixing my senses

Reaching into my mind
to find the hidden "Ahhh..."
I savor only in moments of ecstasy

What is the wonder that it holds?
This hairy nut, seeping opaque milk
like it were a baby's prize tit
awaiting a suckling embrace

As I gaze upon it
I find it lacking in allure
due to its coarse appearance

But the scent,
oh, how I love the scent...

Takes me back to days of youth
caught up in volleyball love
with slippery hands

Against bronze flesh
mingled in tainted pristine sands
I can smell it
as I watch the rolling waves
Passionately lost
in the coconut scents
of a Hawaiian Tropic dream

The Council
Written June 20, 2005

Echoes chime in unison
calling forces of the universe
earth, air, fire and water
all come forward in rebirth

Stirring in harmony
beneath a blaze of blue and gold
streaming like a blanket
to shroud their hidden cove

Elders commence,
Mother Nature and Father Time
join with the Lord and Lady
discussing earth and its demise

Concerns are great
as they scheme and plan
pondering their decision
to destroy or save man

Gazing at this sanctuary
the last plot of perfect earth
they quicken the elements
as the life force, they stir

Hoping their final efforts
shall not falter to waste
lost in the swirl of humanity
that has forgotten, olden ways

Citrus Pie Sacrifice
Written June 24, 2005

Marmalade never enchanted me
with sticky chunks of sweetness
beckoning you to smooth it on

Yet there is was, staring at me

Dreams of some citrus paradise
tempting your tongue to claim it
laying there beneath meringue

Like sun rays through fresh rain clouds

A solid illusion, like Styrofoam
promising to delight the senses
containing you within its warmth

Showering me with a sense of rejuvenation

Striving to melt upon your tongue
leaving the putrid lie of aftertaste
clinging there like a postage stamp

like the zest and zing of a naval orange

Fantasy shattered, you realize
its mask of deceptiveness
the promise of a delightful treat

carrying the sourness of lemon lime

As the bitterness fully claims you
you long to spit it away in disgust
slowly forcing yourself to swallow

teasing me into an eye watering submission

All for a smile upon a wrinkled face
with aged blue eyes that patiently await
loving approval of the gift she's made

blissfully mistaken for tears of sheer delight

High Priest
Written November 2003

Beauty unknown to the most trained eye
coming from places not all can see
power of the spirit fills you up
and you master it so completely

Eyes like flames of emerald
as you venture through the realms
of places most tune out or fear
yet in them you've forever dwelled

Spirits come in droves to bend your ear
people come from far and wide
looking for your steady guidance
listening intently to you advice

Love always has eluded you
not many can truly understand
the voices that keep your mind busy
or the spiritual practices you attend

Lovers come and go
you're too perfect, your light too much
your love too great, your soul too intense
they leave in a daze, feeling inadequate

Lonely you venture, searching for true love
the one that will fill your heart and soul
the love you can only dream of
but can never truly touch

I sit and watch you now
from across the table of our home
observing as the unshed tears stain you
shadowing you for a moment in time

Waiting as the moment fades
like the moon into the horizon
hearing your soul sigh once more
as your light consumes the room

And as the fire spreads to your eyes
you reach and take my hand
to the circle we walk together
once again, as always, best friends

Validation of the Goddess
Written June 21, 2005

Burgundy sheets lie smooth beneath my back
their silk, cooling my naked flesh
As waves of pain bathe me,
imprisoning me in their grip

Watching flames dance upon the wall,
entranced by their candle's silhouettes,
Quietly crying, I softly chant,
awaiting the lunar glow's caress

"Isis, Great Mother,
bless me within your arms,
take away the pain
heal my body, free my spirit
please mend my broken heart"

Mist carrying the scent of jasmine
cover me, instilling inner peace
as golden wings, gingerly claim me
a silken voice, whispers to me

"Daughter of my essence
lay your weary mind to rest
for I am with you always
empowering you, and tonight
I heal you of all you ask"

Bronze fingers, touch my brow in comfort
moving to close my weary eyes
I drift in peaceful sleep, until morning
awaking to the alarm clocks steady hum

And as I stood in hazy thoughts
wondering if she was only a dream,
I began to walk with cat-like movements
realizing, no pain remained in me

Winds gently billowed, sheer gray curtains
silently lulling me their way
as rays of golden light flowed freely
faint scents of jasmine, touched my face

Champagne Bubbles
Written April 9, 2006

From tomorrow, I can see champagne bubbles
shining like tainted ringlets, against cut glass
feeding on the edge of a foundation, cracked

A spider's web guards once hallowed ground
as the recluse patiently eyes a lustful feast
climax beckons the silence of time to breathe

Naked I stretch, testing the fingertips of dawn
A taut nipple caressing threads of defiance
fantasizing a fine mist of carefully spun silk

Cotton candy crevices await feathered strokes
hungry tongues, tweak delusions of the sublime
in the aftermath of tiny fangs, teasing sanity

Tender flesh quivers with promises of afterlife
oblivious to the eight arms of mortality's embrace
destroying flesh long ago denying my escape

As I gaze into froth, fermenting life's desire
scattered pools of existence, waste my sorrow
upon mundane minds of vanity, poised in denial

Feeding on the edge of a foundation, cracked
shining like tainted ringlets, against cut glass
From tomorrow, I can see champagne bubbles

www.ingramcontent.com/pod-product-compliance
Lightning Source LLC
Chambersburg PA
CBHW031942080426
42735CB00007B/231